THE PURSUIT OF TIME *and* MONEY

THE PURSUIT OF TIME *and* MONEY

Time and money often seem finite and limited resources. However, with the right resourcefulness, with the right mindset, our resources can become infinite. This is brilliantly illustrated in *The Pursuit of Time and Money*.

> —**Greg McKeown**, Author of the New York Times
> bestseller *Essentialism: The Disciplined Pursuit of Less.*

A thought-provoking read that helps us to explore the hidden dimensions of time and money and how our internal storylines drive our behaviors. Dr. Spano's ability to bring cutting-edge research to real life application is guaranteed to help you let go of fear and self-sabotaging behaviors so that you can make better life choices. A wonderful book by an extraordinary person. Enjoy.

> —**Nido R. Qubein**, President High Point University.

I can't recommend Dr. Spano highly enough! With a keen understanding of worldview, personal development, entrepreneurial vision and finance, she brings a unique voice to these disciplines. But why money and time?

Dr. Spano writes, *"What if it turned out that everything you believed about time and money was keeping you from achieving a meaningful, prosperous life?"*

Argh, she was right! Dr. Spano's integration of ancient wisdom, modern research, and her global observations helped me write my own, new perspective through the suggested reflective practices. I was immediately drawn into her wisdom regarding time, money and perspective...to the deepest levels of personal understanding. It feels like a new operating system has been installed!

She further reminds, *"Prosperity is a mindset. It's a place to come from—not a place to get to."*

> —**Vernon Rainwater**, Lead Pastor,
> Northland Church, Longwood, Florida

Dr. Sharon Spano has provided the reader with thought-provoking concepts concerning time and money. All of us certainly wish we had more time and more money to achieve our life's goals. Dr. Spano has brought to light that, with proper focus and understanding, we can have an abundance of time and money. Our real happiness lies in other areas. We simply need to think about them differently as Dr. Spano points in this timely book. As a career soldier, I often felt like I needed more time and more money. I wish I had a resource like this book to enable me to understand a better way to grow and experience true abundance.

—Lieutenant General (RETIRED) **Benjamin R. Mixon**

Insightful and practical, Dr. Spano leads you to a heightened awareness of your own personal experience with time and money. Recognizing patterns and behaviors, she provides an effective road map thru "reflective practice" for personal growth and prosperity.

—**James Sang Lee**, 4x ISKA World Martial Arts Champion

Time and money seem to be defined in quite static ways that often imprison us rather than set us on a path to freedom. Sharon Spano's research expands the typical view of time and money as concrete and solid by examining the stories we have about them. How do we transform our views and experiences of time and money from scarcity to abundance and flow? We have heard the notion of scarcity to abundance before, but Sharon's research comes from multiple perspectives including interior, exterior, individual, collective, developmental stages, and states, along with reflective practices. This supports a vivid understanding of how your meaning making and experience of time and money can be a "Cycle of Freedom."

—**Terri O'Fallon**, Ph.D, Founder, Pacific Integral

At last a welcomed and an informed way to look at our personal relationship with time and money.

—**Dick Batchelor**, Dick Batchelor Management Group, Inc.,Business Development Consultant

Living authentically requires knowing our core values and then being true to them: "to thine own self be true," Shakespeare. Dr. Spano utilizes the tools of time and money as a way to explore the essence of who we are, to peer into the windows of our soul. She then provides a transformational process to guide us toward our greater purpose and depth.

Dr. Spano shows how one's deep internal experiences with time and money can sabotage every area of our lives. She points the way toward living with a sense of abundance by providing a transformational process beginning with core beliefs and leading toward our greater purpose. This book encourages and strengthens the essence of living authentically.

—**Martha Mertz**, Founder, Athena International

Building on existing research, Dr. Sharon Spano provides a roadmap for making the transition from a life lived out of a paradigm of scarcity to one of abundance. Through developing a better understanding of and attitude toward our time and money, this volume presents the challenge to live a larger life of stewardship and generosity.

—**Gregory L. Holzhauer**, Law Partner, Winderweedle, Haines, Ward & Woodman, P.A.

This groundbreaking book opens up a new conversation about the pursuit of time and money. Dr. Spano presents a thoughtful, research-based exploration of the paradox of time and money through the lens of human development. Reflective practices at the end of each chapter help us to realize why we may be constrained by our own perspectives of time or money. The good news is—if we are courageous and bold, we can take purposeful steps to improve our chances for a meaningful, abundant life.

—**Gwen DuBois-Wing**, Ph.D., Governance and Leadership Consultant/Coach, DuBois-Wing & Associates

For anyone who's ever experienced the chase for more time and money, this book is a game changer. Dr. Sharon Spano will take you on a thought-provoking journey that will help you explore your beliefs about two of the most important resources in your life. The life application practices really made me think about what it means to pursue time and money in healthier ways.

To the point and very well written. It's very surprising what I found out about myself while reading the book. It's an eye opener.

—**Oliver Tonn**, Co-Owner, Engel & Volkers, Florida, Master License Partner of Engel & Volkers USA Holdings, Inc.

Dr. Spano shows us how time and money are intricately connected windows into the soul of a human being and how they impact both our lives and relationships on a daily basis. One thing I enjoy about Dr. Spano's book is that she doesn't simply stop at awareness but explores how to transition from handcuffs to abundance. I know you will benefit by spending the time and money to glean her wisdom from this book!

—**Caleb Grover** M.A, M.Div, Agape Counseling Center, Licensed Mental Health Counselor

If you are looking for ways to increase profitability or become more efficient, this book is not for you. If, however, you want to discover a transformative pathway to living a life of radical abundance, prosperity, and freedom, then *The Pursuit of Time and Money* is the place to begin.

—**Matthew Simpson**, Founder & Creative Director, Infusion

THE PURSUIT OF
TIME
—— *and* ——
MONEY

STEP INTO RADICAL ABUNDANCE AND DISCOVER
THE SECRET TO A MEANINGFUL PROSPEROUS LIFE

SHARON L. SPANO, Ph.D

NEW YORK

NASHVILLE • MELBOURNE • VANCOUVER

THE PURSUIT OF TIME *and* MONEY
STEP INTO RADICAL ABUNDANCE AND DISCOVER
THE SECRET TO A MEANINGFUL PROSPEROUS LIFE

© 2017 SHARON L. SPANO, PHD

Published in New York, New York, by Morgan James Publishing. Morgan James is a trademark of Morgan James, LLC. www.MorganJamesPublishing.com

The Morgan James Speakers Group can bring authors to your live event. For more information or to book an event visit The Morgan James Speakers Group at www.TheMorganJamesSpeakersGroup.com.

ISBN 978-1-68350-322-4 paperback
ISBN 978-1-68350-323-1 eBook
ISBN 978-1-68350-324-8 hardcover
Library of Congress Control Number: 2016917885

Cover Design by:
Rachel Lopez
www.r2cdesign.com

In an effort to support local communities, raise awareness and funds, Morgan James Publishing donates a percentage of all book sales for the life of each book to Habitat for Humanity Peninsula and Greater Williamsburg.

Get involved today! Visit
www.MorganJamesBuilds.com

To my husband Ralph Spano
For your unconditional love and support and
for blessing me with a life of abundance and joy

To our son Michael
(1981–2008)
Who *was* and *is* the essence of love.

CONTENTS

*Man's search for meaning is the
primary motivation in his life...*
—Viktor Frankl

ACKNOWLEDGEMENTS

No body of creative work is ever started or completed without the express intervention and support of a community. I have been blessed by many. The birth of this book rose out of curiosity as I worked and interfaced with a variety of individuals across multiple disciplines and industries. A special thank you, then, to the many people, on both a personal and professional level, who have crossed my path. Through the years, you have helped me dive into the deeper questions of life.

I also want to acknowledge my husband Ralph Spano for being my biggest fan and for always supporting me through the years of exploring, learning, writing, researching, and deciphering what it means to be complex human beings. You, my dearest friend and companion, are the greatest husband and father a woman could possibly hope for—much more than I deserve.

Additionally, a shout out to Jamie Morris for helping me move through the tedious work of deciphering the structure of this effort. To my editors, Nancy Pile and Nick Pavlidis for fine tuning what was and pointing out what could be. Without the dedication of the three of you, this book would never have come to fruition.

To Robin Reynolds and Amy Sieve for your patience and the endless hours of formatting and administrative support. I would have gone mad without you.

To Terri O'Fallon, Bill Torbert, and Nancy Wallis for awakening me to the many nuances of human development. Your research has opened my heart and changed my life. And, to my colleagues at Fielding Graduate University and Integral Coaching Canada. You know who you are; each of you has enriched my life beyond measure.

Finally, to Pastor Vernon Rainwater, for the difference you make in my life each and every day, for always encouraging me as I unravel my thoughts, and, most importantly, for modeling what it means to walk in love and faith in what is often a complex and confusing world.

Introduction

THE CHASE

What if it turned out that everything you believed about time and money was keeping you from achieving a meaningful, prosperous life?

If you're like many people in today's 24/7 world, you're probably living the chase. The chase is that ongoing, persistent sense of "not being or having enough." No matter how hard you work, there never seems to be enough time to get it all done. And, no matter how much money you make, there's always a surprise demand that pops up to rob you of hard-earned dollars.

My consulting and coaching practice is rooted in the field of human and organizational systems. The ideas and suggestions set forth in this body of work stem from my own exploration and research into how people experience time and money. This initial curiosity began with informal discussions among colleagues and clients wherein I essentially asked two simple questions: What do you believe about time? What do you believe about money? These discussions led to the development of a valid and reliable time/money inventory, which I continue to refine as I engage in deeper qualitative research. Several themes have emerged from this combined body of work, and it is my hope that by sharing these themes in conjunction with my own study, reflections, and field experience, you will develop a deeper understanding of your own experience of time and money. My greater desire is that you'll be more equipped to step into a life of radical abundance so that you can experience a more meaningful and prosperous life.

In my extensive travels around the globe, I have witnessed this chase for time and money, and I've discovered that the chase is a way of being that keeps us from living out our biggest life. Research-based findings in the field of human development, however, tell us that this chase, this way of being, can be changed.

If you feel like you're being held hostage to your calendar and that money is the jailer, this book is for you. If you're tired of this chase, tired of being stressed out and not having the time or money to enjoy the people you love and care about, please know that you can *stop the chase.* You can learn to *pursue time and money* in healthier ways such that you *start living a more meaningful, prosperous life.*

In order to do so, however, transformational change is required. Transformational change is a process. Even when we know we want a different experience of life, we often don't know how to get there. If we want to transform our experience of time and money, we have to consider things we've never considered before. We have to consider changing not only our behaviors but also our world view. We have to choose radical abundance.

This book is designed to help you do just that by taking you on an exploratory journey that will help you move beyond your own chase to a place of radical abundance.

Part I: *The Challenge: Developing Awareness of Your Thoughts and Behaviors*

The journey begins with our addressing the basic dynamics of time and money. This section is designed to help you develop greater awareness about the internal storylines that are driving your behaviors with respect to time and money. Where do you stand in fear and scarcity? Where is there room for growth and improvement?

Part II: *The Vision: Letting Go of the Fear*

Our utilization of time and money serves as a barometer for what really matters to us in life. This section is designed to help you explore where you fall on the spectrum between scarcity and abundance. What are the existing scarcity beliefs that are keeping you from having the life you've always dreamed of? What negative thoughts and emotions are holding you hostage? Where do you need to let go of the fear of not having or being enough?

Part III: *The Opportunity: Stepping into Your Biggest Life*

When we learn to be fully present to our thoughts and behaviors, we can make different choices. We can change the direction of our lives. This section will help you learn how people grow and change so that you can embark on your own developmental path toward freedom and abundance. In developing this capacity, you'll also learn what it means to pursue time and money in healthier ways. How can you mature into your highest potential such that you live your biggest life? What is the secret to freedom from fear and scarcity?

Part IV: *The Solution: Shifting to a Paradigm of Radical Abundance*
When we develop healthier perspectives on time and money, we experience the abundance of life. This section features new ways of being in relationship with time, money, and the people you love. You will learn the secret to a meaningful, prosperous life. What does it mean to live from a Cycle of Freedom™? How can you love from radical abundance such that you experience greater prosperity and joy in your personal and professional lives?

I invite you to embark on this journey and reignite your passion for life. And, here's the good news. Prosperity is in no way dependent on how much time or money you actually have. Prosperity is a mindset. It's a place to come *from*—not a place to get *to*.

Additionally, I hope you'll notice that this book isn't about *managing* time and money. There are thousands of books out there about time and money management. And, yes, with effective management skills you can find more time and perhaps create more money. However, management skills won't necessarily stop the chase. They may, in fact, increase it. This book is about how time and money are windows into the very essence of who you are because how you think about and utilize these two important resources are indicators of what you value most. Ultimately, time and money have the power to dictate your overall experience in life.

The question is, are you living the life you've always dreamed of or is it time to step up your game?

If you're like many people, myself included, there's always space for further growth and development. One of the things I've noticed in my field experience and research on the experience of time and money is that most of us land somewhere on the very nuanced and complex spectrum between scarcity and abundance. By this I mean, we either feel like we have an abundance of time and money or we feel as though there's never enough. But, the nuances don't just end there. If you're like many of the people I encounter in my professional practice, you've probably had the experience of having a lot of time and little money or a lot of money and very little time. This paradoxical relationship between time and money often occurs because we are so busy making money, we don't have the time to enjoy the fruits of our labor. Or, worse yet, we're out of work, so we find ourselves with nothing *but* time.

It's easy to misinterpret the relationship between time and money. If we're not careful, the tension between the two can result in exhaustion, stress, frustration, and in some cases, anger, depression, or other self-destructive thoughts and behaviors. There are very specific reasons for why we cycle between scarcity and abundance. This book explores that conversation in relation to the fear associated with scarcity and the freedom of abundance.

You no longer have to be held captive. You can choose new perspectives that will set you free.

As you maneuver your way through this journey, I also want to encourage you to fully engage in the Reflective Practices outlined at the end of each chapter. Because we are working to develop greater awareness and affect transformational change with respect to your experience of time and money, the timeframes for these practices overlap and extend over the course of many months. This is because the process of growth and development typically occurs over time as we reflect, grow, and change. In other words, you won't be able to complete them as you read through the book. My recommendation is that you read through the book once and then return a second time to engage in the Reflective Practices. You can also download a pdf of the practices from *www.SharonSpano.com* to assist you in this process of discovery.

I also recommend that you keep a journal to record your responses to each of the questions in the Reflective Practices. The intention here is to help you see patterns of thought and behavior so that you can make the necessary changes. These practices are very important to your growth and development because they help you broaden your perspectives. I encourage you to take them seriously and to give yourself enough time to fully engage with the questions.

What you're about to experience in reading this book is vital to how you live out the rest of your life. Boldness is required on my part for this change to occur; courage is required on yours. I invite you to stop the chase and step into your biggest life—a life that allows for greater generosity, gratitude, and compassion—a meaningful and prosperous life that is ultimately fulfilled via purposeful acts of love.

Part I

THE CHALLENGE: DEVELOPING AWARENESS OF YOUR THOUGHTS AND BEHAVIORS

1

THE RELATIONSHIP BETWEEN
TIME AND MONEY

The large room is buzzing with people from all walks of life. The event is a local cocktail party intended to raise money for a worthy cause. People are standing in circles quietly talking about a variety of topics. As I move through the crowd, I listen in and notice that some are discussing politics. Some are reflecting upon the latest news. But a great many of them are talking about what a rough week they've had and how exhausted they are. One person talks about her frustration with the slow service at a local restaurant. A man is worried about the increase in his son's college tuition. A few people in the banking industry are discussing the GNP and the sudden drop in the stock market. I move across the room to another group of people.

There, a woman is speaking about a new position with an increase in salary—a job she can't refuse. This new job requires a move across country. She's not sure how she'll manage a move this dramatic, but she's not at all concerned. "It will all work out," she says. "Things always do." On this side of the room, someone else shares a completely different perspective on the global economy. With confidence, he talks about all things being cyclical. I nod my head and marvel at the many different perspectives.

Clearly, time and money are part of every ongoing conversation in the room, but how is it that some see the glass half empty while others see the glass half full? And, given my own set of circumstances, where exactly does *my* story fall in the conversation?

Listen long and hard enough and you'll quickly see that in this cocktail party called life, people are talking. Not just talking, but are, in fact, driven by time and money. Each and every day of our lives, we're confronted with a variation of this conversation—in one form or another.

If time and money are in our faces this often and with such intensity, it might just be worth your while to pay attention—and not just pay attention, but make a decision as to where you stand on the matter. Although the example here represents a setting with external conversations about time and money, each of us engages in similar internal dialogue on a day-to-day basis. Those internal conversations about time and money can have a profound effect on our overall personal and professional satisfaction. My study and research has identified that those who have more positive internal conversations about time and money may experience greater overall satisfaction and joy. While those who engage in more negative internal conversations about time and money may experience greater stress in every area of their life.

Time and Money are Interrelated

While it may seem as though many of our life conversations are about either time *or* money, research in the field of human development strongly suggests that our experience with time and money may be closely interrelated. One impacts the other in many ways. If I'm chasing time, there's a very good chance that I'm chasing money and vice versa. Much of what we do, say, or experience is impacted by both time *and* money.

So, while time and money are two separate, very different aspects of everyday life, I speak to them as closely connected ideas. My study and research has shown that in their internal conversations about time and money, some people experience the old adage, "time *is* money" in making many daily choices. Throughout most of their days—and lives—these people may experience stress, frustration, and perhaps even the pain of time and money as one aspect of life—a day-by-day experience, if you will, that has the potential to either bring them freedom or catapult them into fear.

Let's go back to that cocktail party. Put yourself in the middle of the room. Which of those conversations would you like to join?

Would you prefer to stand in the conversation that focuses on how you'll never have enough time to get it all done and there's never enough money to do the things you'd love to enjoy? Or, would you prefer to join in the conversation that there is enough—of everything. You have enough time for loved ones, recreation, travel, work, your health, and on the list goes. And, you have enough money to feel safe, secure, generous, grateful, and compassionate towards others? The reality is that both conversations are going on in our minds as we live out our everyday lives whether we realize it or not. Most of us move in and out of these conversations at a subconscious level so often that we rarely notice how easily we're motivated or defeated by this internal dialogue.

Here's the good news. You can *choose* the conversation. You can choose which group of people you prefer hanging out with at this cocktail party called life. And, the even better news is that when you consciously choose that conversation, your reality will change.

Your Perspectives on Time and Money
Can Help You Achieve a Bigger Life

Let's dive a bit deeper then into the source of our internal conversations on time and money and how they influence our lives. The first step is to achieve greater self-awareness and identify your thoughts, emotions, beliefs, and attitudes associated with time and money. In my experience, these aspects dictate your actions and, ultimately, your level of fulfillment because they influence the choices you make and the things you to do or don't do.

Sometimes, this self-awareness makes people uncomfortable or unsure about what's next. That's okay. Any doubts or voices of uncertainty are part of the awareness/discovery process. It's not about beating yourself up for past choices. As I like to remind my clients: *With the first moment of awareness comes opportunity for change.* Without self-awareness, it's often difficult to know what changes to make. This book is designed to help you develop greater self-awareness such that you make the necessary changes.

In fact, my study and research indicates that many people experience internal stress about time and money in some form or fashion. Even those people who feel they generally have a positive internal dialogue on time and money and a healthy approach to life admit to experiencing stress. Becoming self-aware is a powerful first step to minimize those stress points, even for those with a generally positive mindset.

Considering new possibilities and the secret to achieving a deeper, more meaningful life, can help you no matter what your current perspective. We all have room for improvement and new perspectives. Whether you're someone who feels like you're living the chase or you're someone who's got it all together, I can promise you that you can discover new and better ways to experience time and money.

The Chase is Stronger and Faster than Ever Before

Going through the exercises and reflective practices I share with you in this book is more important now than ever before. In this fast-paced world that requires us to respond to every text message, email, phone call, solicitation, and deadline on a second's notice, the question is less about *if* you experience stress, frustration, negative energy, anxiety, and maybe even pain and suffering. The question is now about *how often* are these negative thoughts and emotions running your life?

In the history of the world, I doubt that any group of people has ever felt as driven as those in our society today. Yes, other civilizations have experienced stress about time and money, but that pressure was often limited to demands placed upon them within one isolated town, community, region, state, or nation. Today, the demands of time and money hit us instantaneously on a global level. The Information Age has generated an immediate need for us to have knowledge about everything in an instant, and we're expected to respond immediately or the world moves on without us.

But, that immediacy and interconnectedness also provides never-before-seen opportunities. We can share information faster and to a wider population than ever before. More importantly, research indicates that, as it relates to time and money, you can *choose* to pursue time and money in healthier ways. Again, I'm hoping you'll come to realize that your experience of time and money has absolutely nothing to do with how little or how much time and money you *actually* have. Hold on tightly to this paradoxical premise as we dig deeper into the conversation.

Bottom line: You can change your mind, and in doing so, you can change your life. The promise is a meaningful, prosperous life beyond your wildest imagination.

Reflective Practice:

This first segment of reflective practice is designed to help you develop greater awareness of your thoughts and behaviors in relation to time and money. Chapter 1 focuses on the interrelationship between time and money. This practice is designed to help you pay close attention to your *internal and external dialogue* with respect to time and money.

Over the next seven days, concentrate on at least one scenario each day where you find yourself addressing a time or money situation. For example, maybe while having lunch with a colleague, during a budgetary meeting, or while out shopping with a friend.

At the end of each day, spend 10-15 minutes journaling your responses to the following questions:

- During these situations, what thoughts or emotions surfaced for you in relation to time and/or money?
- What decisions or choices did you make (or not make) as a result?
- How did you feel as a result of the choices you made?
- At the end of the seven days, review your journal entries and take note of any patterns that arose with respect to your experience of time and money.

2

WHY WHAT YOU THINK ABOUT
TIME AND MONEY MATTERS

E verything begins and ends with thought—with cognition. We have to *think* it before we can *feel* or *do* anything.

The car pulls up in front of a house owned by my Aunt Frances and her husband Frank in the suburbs of Los Angeles. They share this house with their three children and my grandmother. My sister and I are being deposited there after my parents' divorce. I am five years old. My paternal grandmother, Isabel, is in charge, with my dad off somewhere in the distance to "live his own life." I'm shown to a room that I'll share with my cousin Norma. I'm now an intruder, a charity case, someone displaced in someone else's home.

This was my cognitive reality. This was how I came to think about who I was in the world. Even at five years old, I knew the stress of isolation and the fear and uncertainty of having parents who didn't have the time or money to invest in me.

9

It began that morning when I was dropped off at Aunt Frances' house—all those early-childhood thoughts and feelings imprinted in my mind a poverty mindset of not being enough. Not belonging. Not having anything of my own. That sense of not belonging and lacking any ownership fractured my identity. What I remember most about that house in La Puente, California, is that it wasn't my home. It was theirs. I would live in that house until the second grade with a small suitcase secretly packed and hidden at the back of the closet. Waiting. Waiting for someone to rescue and claim me as their own.

Distinguished author and executive coach Marshall Goldsmith speaks to our environment as a nonstop triggering mechanism, a stimulus that has the power to reshape our thoughts and actions.[1] We cannot ignore these triggers. They have the power to change how we think and respond. But, in our awareness of the power of these triggers, we can choose to live them out differently. As a young child, I spiraled into a poverty mindset, believing I was not enough because of my external circumstances. Those external circumstances became triggers that shaped the course of my adult life for a great many years. They changed me.

My experience with time and money became clearly defined. What I learned from the stories around me was that neither my mom nor my dad had the time or inclination to care for me. Additionally, my father was one of nine children—my Grandmother Isabel's one and only remaining son. My dad was her favorite, my aunts used to snicker. I was one of Anthony's "brats."

As to money? There was constant dissension between my grandmother and my aunt about my dad's failure to honor his financial commitments for the care of his two charity kids. I remember one occasion when my grandmother packed up her own suitcase, took me by the hand, and together we walked for what seemed like days to the nearest bus stop for a trip to God-knows-where. We were running away together. She and I, on the lam, from all the stress and worry about not being enough. We sat by the side of the road for several hours. I wasn't scared or worried. We were free. I remember the elation in thinking that finally it would be just the two of us. But in the end, my uncle arrived and convinced my grandmother to return to that house of empty promises.

Children need to feel safe, secure, and loved in order to develop self-worth and a sense of abundance. But, remember that our experience of life is dictated by how we make meaning of that experience. People who grow up in homes with loving parents, enough food on the table, and fancy cars can just as easily experience a poverty mindset, albeit for different reasons. Maybe their parents are too busy working to give them full attention. Money may not be the object, but when time is scarce, a child may still experience a deep sense of impoverishment.

Each of us, in our own story, experiences time and money differently. We move in and out of thoughts and behaviors of not being or having enough. Depending on how we've made meaning from our early-childhood stories, we may find ourselves conflicted between thoughts and behaviors associated with fear and scarcity and those associated with freedom and abundance. Our environment, our memories, our external circumstances have the power to shape our internal experience of life—to include how we perceive and utilize our most valuable resources of time and money.

The good news is that the reality of our circumstances does not have to dictate our perspective. We can choose to develop awareness of those stories and their impact on our lives. As we mature, we can choose to make meaning of those stories in ways that offer up a different perspective on time and money and a different sense of identity and self-worth.

How Your Story Fits into the Bigger Picture
of Your Life Experience

The field of human development teaches us that, just as infants generally crawl before they run, we all grow up into specific *stages* of development. Additionally, leading theorists in the field agree upon distinctions between *states, types,* and multiple developmental *lines* that independently arise within each person.[2]

By developmental lines, I'm referring to the cognitive, emotional, somatic, interpersonal, moral, and spiritual dimensions of self. To date, we surmise that each person has at least twenty-four lines of development which help them make sense of the world.[3] Stages, states, lines, and types also come *together* to form who we are as human beings. For the sake of ease, I will refer to these developmental aspects as *dimensions of self.*

Lines of human development cannot be compared to one another,[4] however, they all move in the same direction, that is, developmental lines increase in complexity.

Theoretically, an adult has a more complex understanding of the abstract nature of time and money than does a five-year-old. The common yardstick among all developmental lines is cognition—what we think and understand via our experiences, our five senses, our types (gender, personality, culture, etc.), and the unique ways in which our stages and our developmental lines rise up in complexity. As I mentioned above, a person may exhibit higher levels of cognitive development even as he simultaneously indicates lower levels of moral development. That person might, for example, *know* that something is morally wrong but choose to do it anyway.

According to renowned meta-theorist and author Ken Wilber, "A major reason that the cognitive line is necessary but not sufficient for the other lines is that you have to be aware of something in order to act on it, feel it, identify with it, or need it."[5] Greater self-awareness, then, requires that we pay close attention to our thoughts. How we cognitively make sense of our life experiences impacts how we feel and how we take action. Consider this simple "money" example:

You wake up one morning, deeply concerned about the shortage in your checking account. It's December, the month is half over, and you haven't finished your holiday shopping. You make a firm decision. You'll have to pay extra close attention to your spending in order to complete that shopping list. No extracurricular activities. No self-purchases. No unnecessary movies or dinner with friends. You're committed to staying on budget so that you can buy gifts for the people you care about and love. Later that afternoon, your best friend calls and invites you to the best play on Broadway. He's got the tickets if you'll handle the hotel and your own airfare. You leap at the opportunity without hesitation.

What's changed?

Absolutely nothing. You still have the same amount of money in your account. Payday is still two weeks away. You still have the same number of gifts to purchase. The only thing that changed was your thought process. Somewhere in the midst of the conversation with your friend, you made a decision. It may not have been the best decision, but the point is your thoughts dictated your actions. You may regret your decision later, or you may find a way to create more money to handle any deficit. The point worth noting is that the only thing that changed is the conversation in your own head. We listen to our thoughts as though they're facts—and we make decisions about what to do and what *not* to do—based on those thoughts. It's how we're wired. It's our human nature.

As you can see, our perceptions about time and money are complex and multifaceted. In this book, I am utilizing the tools of time and money as a way for you to explore who you are and what really matters most to you in your life. Our early childhood stories are but one factor in how we think about and ultimately utilize time and money.

Researchers Argyle and Furnham remind us that there is "a clinical, cognitive, developmental, differential, and experimental psychology of money."[6] Further research indicates that even though parents rarely talk about money with their children, we acquire many of our monetary attitudes and habits directly from our parents at an early age.[7]

I invite you to reflect on your earliest childhood memories as one way to discover where you are now. We'll use these memories as a cornerstone for much of our further discussion on time and money. When we come to more fully understand how our past stories and our present internal conversations work for or against us with respect to time and money, we can begin to make more informed choices.

Reflective Practice:

This chapter focuses on the *cognitive line of development* and how we make meaning from our early childhood stories. This practice is designed to help you reflect upon one or two early childhood stories in relation to time and money. Spend a minimum of 30 minutes mapping out your story in your journal. Write out as many details as you can remember and include anything from your five senses and any feelings you can recall. Then, answer the following questions in your journal:

- Who were the main characters in your story?
- What were the conversations you remember hearing about time? About money?
- What were the conclusions you came to as a result of the conversations around you?
- How do those memories impact your choices and decisions with respect to time and money in the present time?

3

THE PARADOX OF
TIME AND MONEY

s I mentioned earlier, time and money are interrelated and our experience of both may be directly related to our early childhood stories and our existing dimensions of self. Given these contentions, we have a unique opportunity to grow up into new perspectives. We can adopt a new way of being. We can recreate our relationship with time and money. We can improve how each of those resources impacts our daily lives.

Implementing a process to broaden our perspectives on time and money is often a gradual one. However, it is one that builds momentum as we *wake up* to the potential within our own dimensions of self by way of stages, states, and lines of human development. I will discuss this potential in more depth in a later chapter. For now, let me say that the more we understand about our own potential for growth, the more we will come to understand how our time and money mindsets were formed and how we can change them. If our goal is to ultimately live a more meaningful, prosperous life, we must be wise enough to engage in the work to be done. Even so, changing our assumptions and behaviors about two resources so vital to our daily way of life is not a journey without challenge. Both time and money are paradoxical in that there is a contradictory tension that inherently exists between them, a tension that we run up against in our daily life whether we realize it or not. This tension only adds to our challenge. In my work in the field, I have come to note this tension in three specific ways that may help you further unlock new perspectives.

Tension No. 1: *Time and money are both concrete and abstract.*
Let's first talk about money . . . It doesn't take an economist to quickly figure out that money is both concrete and abstract all at once. Yes, we have a daily concrete experience of money in that we handle, exchange, earn, and spend some form of currency that we can see and touch. However, there is an abstract nature associated with money because it's value is often rooted in some form of abstract theoretical, conceptual, or philosophical ideal, e.g., political ideologies, ever-fluctuating markets, the threat of terrorism and war, and overall global uncertainty.

Allow me to suggest that it's this tension between the concrete and abstract nature of money that often makes our daily life stressful and challenging. On a macro-level, we can look, for example, to the many variations of currency across the globe. Based on abstract ideals, money has a different numerical value from one country to another.

For example, there are currently 180 currencies recognized as legal tender in the United Nations' member states alone. Imagine having to know and understand the exchange rate between a Russian ruble and an Afghan afghani. I have enough trouble converting a dollar to a euro. Then, there's the pound, the kwanza, the peso, the taka, and the list continues: mark, boliviano, kyat, yuan, colon, guilder, koruna, quetzal, gourde, forint, shekel, dinar, rand, rupee, and on it goes. A pound in Great Britain does not necessarily have the same value as a pound in Egypt.

Why?

Because the value of each unit of measure is different based on the complex and ever-changing market at the national and global levels. Have one economy collapse like we witnessed in Greece in 2010 and the years that followed, and the rest of Europe experiences a domino effect. Even when that domino effect isn't hard and fast, one economy impacts another.

For the average citizen, no matter what nationality, the ever-changing market rarely makes sense. We're just trying to keep up. All we really know is that the price of tomatoes may be more in Europe than they are in the United States—according to the exchange rate—but it's all relative. Europeans flock to U.S. outlet malls to stock their suitcases with lower-priced Uggs, and Americans wonder, "What's the big deal?"

Add ongoing war to the mix or a sudden change in world leadership, and people start to get really fearful about the value of their money. Remember learning about the quick demise of the Confederate dollar after the Civil War? If you were on the losing side, those concrete, spendable dollars quickly became nothing more than a paper memory.

If you think our experience of money isn't emotional, consider the cost of housing, transportation, food, utilities, and entertainment in countries like Italy where any Italian on the street will quickly share how they're working more for less money. As one gentleman outside Florence told me, the transition to the euro has caused them to lose at least 40 percent of their wealth.

So it is across the world as each and every country struggles with its own economy and the impact of a global society. Money is abstract, yes, but it impacts us every day in very concrete ways. Is it any wonder, then, that we spend so much time talking about the effects of money on our daily life? It isn't hard to imagine that a big part of our stress and worry is linked to the abstract and concrete nature of money. If we're not careful, all of these factors can drive us in the direction of fear and scarcity.

The point of this discussion is not to increase your worry but to help you understand the very nature of money such that you can learn to master your experience of it. But, before we go there, let's take a look at the nature of time.

Time is equally concrete and abstract (and no less frustrating). We have clocks and watches and phones that buzz us when it's time to rush off to an afternoon appointment. I happen to be one of those people who love clocks. I collect them, in fact, but I have to admit that of the twenty-plus clocks in my home, only two are actually wound. The grandfather is one because I love the sound of the clock striking the hour (except at midnight). The other is a cuckoo clock that my husband and I purchased in Germany. I love the sound of its music because it reminds me of that wonderful afternoon in the Black Forest as we perused the most amazing clock shop I'd ever seen.

All this to say, I love the concrete aspect of time as it's expressed via an antique or aesthetically-pleasing physical clock or watch. I'm not, however, a big fan of time itself. If you're like me, you probably feel constrained by time. There are never enough hours to get it all done. On any given day, if I'm not careful, I can feel like I'm being stalked by the clock. I have way too many things to do, the clock keeps ticking, and time is running out. I've learned to master this sense of not having enough time, but it has been a long process.

In our westernized worldview, time *is* money. We work harder and longer. But, it wasn't always like this. Once upon a time, before the Industrial Revolution, America was an agrarian society. People worked and played hard, but they lived by the seasons and the rising and setting of the sun. Most likely, they did so with a far lesser sense of being chased by the clock. So, when did this chase begin?

When Abstract Time Becomes Concrete Money

How is it that the abstract nature of time came to equate to money? History tells us that the chase began at the turn of the 20th century when Frederick Taylor introduced Scientific Management.[8] Taylor, one of the most influential men of his era, conducted time and motion studies that served as the cornerstone for work design in manufacturing. The underlying premise of these studies was based on five principles that essentially reduced the workforce to robots. All operations were scientifically broken down, analyzed, and standardized. Managers were to do all the thinking; workers were to execute the designated tasks. Efficient production measured against the clock resulted in increased productivity and greater profits.

Clearly, no one can deny the importance of increased productivity and greater profits. All was good except for the fact that these increases robbed the workforce of autonomy, and in some cases, self-worth. People's work ethic became measured by the clock. Their value was determined by how much they could produce by quitting time. Whereas the pre-industrialized farmer or local shopkeeper might work longer hours out of duty and responsibility to his customers, crops, livestock, and family, the factory worker might work even longer hours out of fear of losing his job. While his pay might be more constant than the farmer or the local entrepreneur, he no longer had control of his work efforts. This shift from farm-to-factory mentality drastically influenced many things in our culture to include our experience of time. The abstract nature of time soon equated to money and with this newfound sense of time, work was often reduced to meaningless tasks and a life of drudgery.

In our modern-day work culture, we can thank Taylor for the mechanization of systems and processes that have produced standardized ways of doing business. Everything from the cut of a McDonald's French fry to how we handle insurance claims and select the best NFL players is designed to be efficient and profitable. Productivity is measured by how many claims you can respond to in an hour or how many burgers you can flip and turn. Taylor's time and motion studies, it seems, did more than just increase productivity and profits. The mechanization of the workforce, across multiple disciplines, was the beginning of a social trend that essentially involved the mechanization of life itself.[9]

The Information Age and an increase in corporate structures have only added to our frustrated experience of time and money. Today, many of us may not be forced to punch a time clock, but the expectations on our time are often far greater.

I can remember being a young administrative assistant for one of the largest law firms in downtown Los Angeles. Before FedEx and emails, we had to depend on airmail (might as well have been carrier pigeons) to get documents from Los Angeles to New York. The beauty of this delay was that it gave us time to gather information or redraft needed documents while we awaited a response from clients or colleagues across the country.

Next came something that looked like an iron lung machine. It was the earliest version of a fax machine, only the size of a small refrigerator. I remember it was enthroned on a conference table in a separate room of its own. We would stand around in awe as a document slowly came through.

Yes, we worked hard. We worked very long hours, but I honestly believe that because we had less distractions, we were more efficient than a worker today who is expected to respond to emails, voicemails, or text messages on a moment's notice. Today, if we fail to immediately respond to a need or query, decisions are made, and people move on. There's no time to process all the information needed in order to make an informed choice or decision as there once was.

The pressure of time is only increasing. While modern technology is designed to offer us a concrete and abstract experience of time in ways that help us increase our productivity, one has to wonder the impact this immediate response cycle will have on existing and future generations.

I was recently on a conference call where one Gen Xer commented, "We have no time to breathe. People in my generation move from one idea or task to another with little time to enjoy the moment. We're forced to keep up with work, family, and friends in real time, and it's exhausting."

Just think about it. How many times throughout your day do you take a quick glance at your watch or the clock on your computer to determine the time? More importantly, at the end of every day, do you feel that you accomplished a lot or a little? So, we run faster and faster because the abstract nature of time, at least in the westernized context of business, equates to money. But, is this true of other cultures?

No Alarm Clocks in Africa?

The abstract and concrete nature of time can look quite different if you live in a small, indigenous village in Africa versus the hustle and bustle of New York or Chicago. Time is valued and respected differently in cultures that are less industrialized. When I think of the abstract nature of time, I think of other cultures and the fact that time is relative. Many questions arise.

For example, there are those who believe that people who live in the southern-most parts of the world, where the weather is hot, move slower than people who live in the rest of the world. These people are seemingly less urgent about time than are people buzzing about Milan or Boston. Obviously, we all have the same number of hours in the day, but is it possible that cultures that live and thrive in hotter climates experience time differently?

Or, what about daylight savings time? Most of North America and parts of Europe decisively advance the clocks by one hour so that evening daylight is one hour longer. Does this extended daylight cause us to experience time in more leisurely ways? Does the perception of a longer day help us feel as though we actually have more hours?

The abstract nature of time is subtly experienced in a variety of ways. I recall a recent experience my husband and I had at the Dubai International Airport. While attempting to get from one side of the airport to another, we were routed first to a train and then onto a small shuttle bus. My husband and I exchanged sideway glances as the driver ever-so-slowly maneuvered his way through the backdrop of the larger airport. I couldn't help compare the ten-mile-an-hour pace with what I've witnessed in American terminals. As the 90-plus-degree sun beat through the shuttle window, I remember thinking that we were probably going to miss our flight even though we'd allowed over an hour to make the connection. No one was in the slightest rush. My husband began to grow anxious. Time was wasting, after all.

No sooner had we shared another sideway glance, then our shuttle was hit broadside by a man driving a smaller golf-cart-type vehicle. After a very loud bang, our driver calmly got out of the shuttle. There was no yelling or screaming, but for the next twenty minutes at least fifteen men gathered from out of nowhere to stop and stare at the damage done to our vehicle. Everyone was calm; no one seemed pressed for time or in the slightest bit concerned about rushing us onto another shuttle so that the passengers could make their respective connections. As my husband and the other westernized passengers sat awestruck by the lack of urgency, I silently marveled at these men who didn't seem in the least bit concerned about time. Time, it seemed, stood still. They were completely immersed in the moment, quietly chatting about the accident.

Finally, a supervisor arrived and called another shuttle. The clock kept ticking, but no one seemed to care that we were, after all, in an airport, and, as passengers, quite likely to miss our flights. One American woman was so outraged by their lack of attention to time, that she gave the supervisor an earful when we finally disembarked from the damaged shuttle. Dare I say that the next shuttle driver, going no more than the prescribed ten-miles-per-hour, carefully wound his way up, down, over, and across the airport. He also demonstrated little to no concern about our "time" schedule.

Over an hour later, we arrived at our terminal. It was one of those scenarios that you had to witness firsthand to believe. By this time, my husband was outraged by the lack of urgency. Being a student of time and money, however, I found the entire scene quite fascinating. I enjoyed the contrast between the "Dubai" experience of time and what I imagined might have happened in a similar scenario at Kennedy or La Guardia.

While I can't attest to this "stress-less" sense of time for all citizens of Dubai, I can also say that I experienced a similar abstract, carefree nature of time while visiting Costa Rica some years ago.

Is it possible that in places like Dubai or Costa Rica, the combination of sun and water influences how people experience the abstract nature of time? Italians might agree since they've been engaged in an ongoing debate about people from the south of Italy being far less ambitious and industrious than those in the north.

Let's take a look at the Costa Rican experience of time in particular.

Costa Rica: La Vida Pura Experience of Time

Truth be told, my husband and I seriously considered moving to Costa Rica a few years ago because we were frankly exhausted. Beyond the beautiful people and the amazing beaches, what we saw in Costa Rica was the opportunity for a simpler life-- one that demanded less of our time and money.

Costa Rica is one of those places that still somewhat qualifies as a "developing country." Dirt thoroughfares, an emerging infrastructure, and cows in the middle of the road are part of the charm. The country is certainly not underdeveloped in that tourists can enjoy the amenities of westernized industrialization. Even so, the charm of the "vida pura" way of life, as the locals like to say, is a "pure life" that is simplistically appealing.

My husband and I marveled at a traffic jam between cows roaming down the middle of a dirt road and the latest BMWs stuck amidst tourist vans. No one honked their horn or waved their fist in frustration because both locals and tourists alike understand that the intersection between these two worlds is part of the wonder of vida pura. No rush. No worry. No place to go that can't wait.

Take one early-morning walk along one of Costa Rica's pristine beaches, and you're lost in time. But, when you've lived in an inner city of noise, traffic, and chaos, a big part of me wondered, could I even manage the slower pace? You see, the complexities of time and money and our experience of them are ingrained in who we are. I, for example, am a "city" girl. I thrive on a lot of activity, and I use my time and money accordingly. The slower-paced experience of life in Costa Rica probably wouldn't suit me for very long.

Most of us make choices based on the concrete and abstract nature of time whether we realize it or not. This is precisely why I contend that if we're chasing money, we're more than likely chasing time, and vice versa. The two constructs go hand in hand when it comes to our experience and the emotions associated with those experiences.

Ask yourself the question: When I do make time, in-person (not via social media), for family and friends, do I experience emotions of guilt, shame, or frustration as an outcome of such choices?

If you find yourself answering yes to this question, chances are you're experiencing the tension between the concrete and abstract nature of time.

Tension No. 2: *Our Perception of Time Can Create Our Reality.*
If you're sitting at a stoplight, late for work, seconds seem like hours.
Why? Because you're stressed for time. You're in a hurry to get where
you're going. Every second is precious. But, if you're sitting at that
same traffic light, and you're hoping to read and respond to a text or
email, the light seems to suddenly turn green. You're then frustrated
because the clock seemed to move too quickly.

Then there's the old adage that time seems to move more quickly
when you're aging. The concrete aspect of time, as in there are only 24
hours to every day, doesn't really change. How, then, could it possibly
move more quickly as we age?

My theory is that time seems to move more quickly as we age
because we tend to focus more on the little time left. In other words,
we're staring at the clock of our own lifespan. In middle school, as you
look to college or the perceived freedom of adulthood, the lifespan ahead
looks long and far away. At age 70, however, the lifespan ahead is much
shorter, so it appears as though time is moving too quickly. Unless, of
course, you're experiencing a critical illness or long for a lost loved one.

At some point in life, most of us have had the experience of time
standing still as we watch someone we love suffer or transition through
the end of life. Then, once they have passed on our reality of time shifts
yet again. On some days, the longing is so deep, it can feel as though
they have been gone forever. Then, suddenly, you wake one day to realize
that your loved one has now been gone for years and years.

Depending on the nature of our circumstances, our age, our role in
life, the demands upon us, the number of people we love and serve—all
of these variables and a host more determine our experience of time.

Let's take a look at yet another perspective on the paradoxical nature
of time and money.

Tension No. 3:

The tension between the concrete and abstract nature of time and money impacts our emotions, perceptions, and behaviors.

Money is a key component in our lives because it quite literally is the resource or tool we exchange for goods and services. How we think about and utilize that tool impacts our emotions and our experience of life. And since we've agreed that we will talk about time and money as a unified concept, let's assume that how we think about money also impacts our emotions and behaviors associated with time.

A weekend in Las Vegas, Nevada is a perfect example of how the existing tension between time and money impacts our emotions, perceptions, and behaviors. This reality is precisely the reason commercials advertising Las Vegas promote it by suggesting "What happens in Vegas, stays in Vegas." The entire city is designed to have us lose track of time and money so that we can experience the "high" associated with the "freedom" from the constraints of time and money. When people experience that manufactured high, they throw reason out the window and indulge. Vegas is an adult Disneyland blueprint that would have us live in a fantasy world where time and money are of no consequence. When we're in those casinos, we move about free of the constraints of time and money—or, at least that's the story marketers would have you believe.

But, we're never really free of time and money, are we?

In order to maintain the fantasy, casinos are designed to offer illusion. Why do you think you're given chips instead of real dollar bills? It's far easier to throw responsible behavior out the window when you're playing with fake money. And, even chips are now becoming obsolete as more and more gaming options are digital. If there's no real physical exchange of money, it's easier to convince yourself that you're not throwing away your hard-earned paycheck. This is the same premise underlying credit cards. It's also far easier to lose track of time when there are no windows or clocks in the casinos. And, is it my imagination, or does the MGM Grand smell like money? You walk through the door, and it's all there for the taking.

Since I'm originally from Los Angeles, weekends in Las Vegas were something I was familiar with from an early age. I can remember my first trip to Las Vegas as a young woman. My husband and I drove over with another couple ready for a weekend of fun in the sun. Dare I say, we never made it poolside. On that first night, we went to dinner and a show. There's nothing quite as exciting as coming out of a Vegas show out onto the gambling floor in an evening gown. The gambling tables are swarming with people, the room is buzzing with excitement. Drinks are flowing. When you're twenty-one, it's an adventurous scene.

We gambled for what seemed like a few hours. You can imagine my shock when we walked out of the casino to grab a cab and my eyes were slammed shut by daylight. I'll never forget it. I couldn't believe that we had been out an entire night. But, when you have dinner at 9:00 and a show that lets out at midnight, time evaporates.

I was hooked. Vegas was happening. Yes, our emotions ran high. We had a pocket full of chips. It was a glamorous, exciting evening. But, when I later asked my husband how much money I'd lost on that one turn of the roulette wheel, and he told me about a hundred dollars, the reality hit. I could have used that money toward my car payment or some other necessity. I remember thinking, what had I done? Guilt and shame set in.

My emotional stance of fun and freedom gave me a false sense of security. You see, Vegas offers a surrealistic experience of time and money. It's glamorous, fun, and exciting. Most of us can experience the fun of Vegas every now and then without going overboard. I enjoy the shows, the food, the shopping. I can take or leave the gambling. For me, it's just a game, and I can easily walk away.

But, the emotions and behaviors would be very different if I were a compulsive gambler, if I'd lost an entire month's worth of income. Sometimes our emotional desires can change our thinking. When this happens, we might behave in ways that get us into trouble. Those behaviors can, thereby, produce more negative emotions, and the cycle continues. Take, for example, a cycle of compulsive gambling.

Compulsive gambling is an illness and an extreme example of how our emotions about time and money impact behaviors. As in any social disease, there are obviously underlying psychological reasons for compulsive gambling. A compulsive gambler is emotionally attached to the high of gambling. It's not about the money. A compulsive gambler will actually keep playing until he loses. He is addicted to the highs and lows of the game and can lose track of time and throw caution to the wind. When the compulsive gambler wins, he or she is high and just as excited as I was on that first trip to Las Vegas. The difference is, the compulsive gambler keeps playing until all that money disappears. Then, he's filled with remorse, guilt, and shame until he or she can muster up enough time and money to play again.

I've personally experienced a similar, though far less devastating, example of remorse and shame that occurs after an ill-planned shopping sprees. In my case, I might spot the perfect suit or an amazing pair of shoes, and my perceptions immediately become momentarily clouded. My emotions take over, and the result is irresponsible spending. When I spontaneously succumb to the temptation of such a purchase, guilt usually hits me before I get the bags in the car. In these scenarios, I've used a credit card–an abstract source of money–and, thus, rarely feel the pain of the purchase in the moment. But the reality of a concrete bill yet to come usually knocks me back into reality by the time I get home. It's a cycle that many women admit to having experienced.

We are vulnerable to our perceptions if they are not grounded in some deeper understanding of the dimensions of self. When we respond to our perceptions in harmful or self-destructive ways, we experience negative emotions.

By contrast, when we have healthy perspectives about time and money, we can responsibly gamble, shop, travel, offer up amazing gifts to charity, or do pretty much whatever we want because, for the most part, we have some level of control over our thoughts, emotions, and behaviors. Win, lose, or draw, we're free of negative stressors associated with time and money. We have a different mindset that results in different emotions and behaviors. We give ourselves permission to let time slip away or spend and share those dollars because we're aware and prepared. Irresponsible behavior is not a way of life. We experience positive emotions as a result of this awareness and our preparedness.

We must, however, be ever aware of our vulnerability when it comes to our experience of time and money. When we have things happen in life that make us feel out of control, our emotions are impacted in a negative way, and our resultant behaviors may look very different. A middle-income bank teller may feel that she's living a balanced, economically sound life until she loses her job. A homeless man may be grateful for one meal a day at a local shelter until that shelter closes down. At any given moment, we can experience emotions attached to either having too much time and money or not enough. The difference is in how we think about what we have. Life changes, and when it does, our thoughts, emotions, and resultant behaviors change to accommodate our experience. When we believe we are safe and have enough, our emotions and behaviors will be very different than when we believe that there is a shortage of time and money.

But, what is enough? Does a billionaire, with all her duties and responsibilities to employees, shareholders, and family, feel more or less stress and frustration on a daily basis than a single mother with three children who works two jobs?

The contrast seems obvious. Each of us would most likely answer—yes, the emotions of fear, anxiety, and stress would be far greater for the single mother because she has fewer options and less resources. The universal truth is—it's all relative.

We share one commonality regardless of our circumstances. We think about time and money on a daily basis because we need these resources to survive and even thrive. Whether we have a lot or a little, we're driven by our needs. Whether we're experiencing a fun weekend in Vegas, trying to keep a billion-dollar business afloat, or food on the table, we experience emotional tension between the concrete and abstract aspects of time and money. Those emotions impact our behaviors.

What we believe about time and money is directly related to how we understand our experience of life. Understanding the basic premise of this tension is the first step to a more meaningful, prosperous life.

Tension No. 4:
How we utilize time and money impacts our relationships.

This factor is a key component to our discussion in that how we decide to use our time and money is indicative of what we most value. We'll give more of our time and money to causes we care about and to people we love. There's little chance that you'll contribute to a charity that you're not interested in or that you'll volunteer at the local animal shelter if you have zero tolerance for dogs. What matters to your heart is where you'll place your treasures.[10] How much time and money I give or share with others is something I want to be aware of because it alerts me to the condition of my own heart.

Remember my own story of me as little girl with the packed suitcase? The fact that my parents didn't have time or money to invest in my care and well-being spoke volumes to how they valued me in their lives. As a young child, I didn't understand the subtle nuances of their failure to provide, but I can honestly say that their lack of responsible parenting dramatically impacted my self-worth. It took years to unravel that unworthiness, and I'm not sure that I would have ever been able to do so had my husband not been the supportive, nurturing, loving man that he is. He has invested his time and money in me in countless ways throughout the years. This investment is a constant reminder of how much I am loved and appreciated. How we share and distribute our most valuable resources alerts others to how we value them in our life.

In fact, this is precisely why a wife gets angry or feels slighted when her husband misses a birthday or anniversary. It's truly not the gift that matters. Rather, she has a perception that her husband did not take the time to remember the event or to make a gesture of giving and appreciation. It's the thought behind the gift that shows his love. A woman wants to know that her husband took time out of his busy life to do something that would bring her joy. If he buys her a blender when she's mentioned four times that she'd love a new pair of earrings, she's going to be hurt and disappointed. She's not upset because she doesn't appreciate that her husband noticed a new blender was needed. She's upset because her husband failed to notice something that may have mattered to her more. Spending the time to consider what *she* would truly value communicates love. It communicates your heart.

Our relationships have to do with the heart. How we feel and love. Throwing expensive gifts at someone isn't the answer either if those gifts come from a shallow heart. The point is to examine your heart and your relationships, and ask yourself, "Am I willing to give my most valuable resources to this person or to this cause?"

Reflective Practice:
This chapter focuses on the paradoxical tensions that exist between time and money. This reflective practice is designed to help you develop awareness as to how the nature of time and money impacts your *emotions and your relationships with others.* Once you've completed the practices

outlined in earlier chapters, I recommend you spend at least two weeks observing how you think and respond to key people in your life with respect to your use of both time and money.

Pay attention to your daily interactions with others and select one instance each day where you notice something arising around the use of time and/or money. Observe yourself in this interaction, and then spend 15-20 minutes journaling responses to the following questions each evening:

- What is your relationship with the person(s) in the specific encounter you had today?
- How did one of the tensions between time and money play into the interaction?
- What were the emotions, perceptions, or behaviors you demonstrated with respect to time or money?
- How did your response seem to impact your relationship with the other person(s)?
- How did you feel about the outcome?

Part II

THE VISION: LETTING GO OF THE FEAR

4

TIME AND MONEY AS A
WINDOW INTO YOUR SOUL

I mentioned in the Introduction that time and money are windows into the essence of who you are. I have also offered that our utilization of time and money indicates what we value most, including how we value and invest our time and money on others. Given these two heavy-weight contentions, let me now add that what I'm really suggesting is that time and money are a window into our very souls. Our utilization of these two resources is an indication of our character and our moral and spiritual development. One doesn't have to look too far beyond the debacles of Wall Street in 2008 to understand the truth of this reality.

Once we come to understand where we fall in the spectrum between scarcity and abundance as it relates to our early childhood stories and our current dimensions of self, we can begin to create a bigger life. The purposes of this chapter is to help you reconsider where you are in terms of your own spiritual and moral lines of development and how these two lines of development relate to your experience with time and money. When we consider this particular element of self-discovery in the context of time and money, we not only resolve any scarcity perspectives that may exist within us, we also open up the doorway to a deeper, richer, more meaningful experience of life in general.

Few people consciously think about time and money in relation to their own spiritual or moral development. Research in the field, however, points to the fact that people in the early developmental stages, (more about this in a later chapter) to include their spiritual and moral lines of development, may find themselves especially challenged by time and money issues because they haven't developed as strong a capacity to learn from the past or project into the conceptual future. If we consider the ramifications of this, it is worth our time and effort to explore ways to develop our spiritual and moral dimensions of self.

Whatever your spiritual or moral values and beliefs, how you live out your daily life impacts every other dimension of self. Remember, your developmental lines are all interconnected. We have a choice to remain stagnant in our development of these lines, or we can choose to engage in practices that support greater awareness and self-improvement.

A more common way to consider this interconnection lies in our pop culture's discussion surrounding the relationship between mind, body, and spirit. For instance, if I have an internal dialogue telling me that I'm too weak to run a marathon, there's very little chance that I'm going to get my body out of bed every morning at 5:00 am to train. In this case, my sense of self is that I am too weak to compete.

Whether we describe these dimensions of self in terms of developmental lines or in the more common phraseology of mind, body, and spirit, we can likely agree that many traditions speak to some component of this triangular relationship that exists within us. We are not just mind, nor body, nor spirit. We are a combination of all three.

Time and money, as vital components of our everyday world, impact our spirit, or what some traditions refer to as our "soul." This is important to our discussion on time and money because our soul can stand as representative of all the dimensions of self as we've described them. It is our energy, our field of consciousness, if you will, and it reflects the very core of who we are. In her book *The Soul of Money*[11], for example, Lynne Twist speaks to the reality that we often diminish or compromise our own soul when we have an unhealthy relationship with money. Look at the death and destruction around us as a result of greed, and it's not too difficult to imagine. Let me add that this is also true for our relationship with time.

We must come to face the fact that the stressors of time and money have the potential to disintegrate the mind, body, and spirit. We fight a battle between our need for wholeness and integration and our egocentric desires. By egocentric desires, I mean, any and all desires that result in a splintered self or that are harmful to ourselves and others.

The duality is this: we are designed to be wholly integrated, but it is also our human nature to desire things that are harmful. Add to this nature the fact that many of us have "roots" or childhood experiences that are unhealthy, and you have within a broken self that is expressly set up for failure.

When we're splintered or fragmented, for whatever reason, we are vulnerable to our own curiosity and unhealthy desires. We behave in ways that feed our need to have more, be more, or to have power and control over others. Or, we seek unhealthy approval. On a micro level, it's that place in our hearts that allows for anger, conflict, and greed. On a macro level, it's the place that creates division, war, famine, destruction, and terrorism. No matter what the setting, these internal and external battles are prevalent in our society. With gangs, it's often a battle between territory and honor. With Wall Street, it's a battle between the rich and the middle class or poor. In religion, it's a battle between good and evil, or "sin." Psychologists speak to this process as fragmentation or our shadow side. I will use the word "transgression" because, although the word "transgression" is often associated with a spiritual wrongdoing, it encompasses a broader perspective in that the path to disintegration is a path against codes of good conduct in any context—from offenses against self, others, and, yes, in the religious context, ultimately against God.

It doesn't matter the context in which you find yourself experiencing a disintegration of self. What matters is that you nurture the developmental progress of your spiritual and moral lines. To do so recognizes that there is indeed a battle raging in our internal world, and it's impacting our external society. That battle doesn't just exist on our flat screens or in our neighborhood streets and cities. The battle isn't some fantasy *Star Wars* or *Harry Potter* movie. It's real, and it exists in the hearts and minds of each and every one of us. Time and money are simply the weapons by which we engage in or fight this battle. They serve as our expressions of either freedom or fear.

Up until now, we've been talking about thoughts, emotions, perceptions, and beliefs, and how all of these dimensions of self potentially impact our behavior in positive and negative ways. When all of these parts of who we are come together in an integrated way, we experience freedom. We are whole.

Integrating Your Mind, Body, and Spirit: A Practical Example

One of the simple challenges I face on a regular basis involves chocolate milkshakes. My brain/body craves a chocolate milkshake because my blood sugar is low. I'm on the way to the dry cleaners, and the mantra of desire rings over and over again in my head: "Stop at Chick-fil-A. They have the best milkshakes, and it's right next-door to the dry cleaners."

My mind says, "No. You can't have a milkshake. You know it's bad for you. You don't need those extra calories, and you definitely don't need to elevate your blood sugar."

If my spirit and my willpower are strong in that moment, I avoid the milkshake. But if my spirit is depleted because I'm feeling tired or particularly stressed out, I can just as easily lack the self-discipline to make a good choice. When this happens, there's a good chance you'll find me standing at the counter ordering that milkshake before you can whisper the word, "Chocolate."

Imagine this same battle a hundred times over for someone who's struggling with addiction or a mental or critical illness. The challenges they face are enormous. No matter what the challenge, when the spirit is broken, the battle is immediately lost.

Whatever the reason for the battle within, integration of the mind, body, and spirit is part of the necessary process required for us to achieve deeper levels of fulfillment and meaning in our lives.

Developing Your Spiritual Line: A Brief Exploration

Bestselling author John Ortberg likens the soul/spirit, which he uses interchangeably, to a computer, calling it the operating system of the body.[12] He further describes the importance of soul in a precise and meaningful way within the context of four concentric circles. Allow me to paraphrase his teaching because it's useful to our discussion on the importance of developing the spiritual and/or moral lines of development.

Ortberg positions the will in the innermost circle. It represents our capacity to choose, and in our discussion throughout this book, we've been talking about how we choose ways to utilize our resources of time and money. We can choose to use these resources wisely, or we can choose to squander them. We can choose abundance over scarcity; we can elect to live a life of freedom or a life based on fear of "not enough."

According to Ortberg, the will is great at helping us with small, everyday decisions, but when it comes to helping us break through belief systems, habits, egocentric desires, attitudes, and patterns that are rooted deep within who we are, the will can often fail us.

The next circle is represented as the mind. The mind represents our thoughts, feelings, and awareness—conscious and subconscious. The mind craves peace, but the will isn't strong enough to help in that regard, so when desires of the "flesh" get in the way, the mind will give in. I speak to these desires as transgressions, which may lead to unhealthy behavior patterns that result in disintegration. Ortberg contends that such actions damage the soul.

The next circle is represented as the body. Here again, we are filled with "appetites" and "habits" all of which equate to behaviors—anything from a love of cheeseburgers to the habit of driving a car or the learned behavior of squandering time and money.

Then, finally, the outermost circle, within which all other aspects of self are contained, is the soul. The soul, Ortberg explains, is designed to seek "harmony, connection, and integration"[13] between our will, mind, and body. We are intricate creatures of amazing design, and in the brilliance of this design, we are integrated, yet broken and fragile, and we crave something beyond ourselves.

When we're broken or fragile, we make decisions about our time and money in fear; we then produce scarcity and more fear. Fear can catapult us into behaviors contrary to our own well-being. We may even self-medicate in one form or another to mask the fear or to fill the abyss of loneliness and isolation. We may use our money on all the wrong things, or we may spend our time with all the wrong people. The list of how we use time and money to manifest our fear is endless.

To reiterate, how we think about and utilize our time and money has a direct impact not only on our mind and body but also on our very soul. We are caught up in a battle between the disintegration and integration of that very soul, but we can choose the path of integration and by doing so, create the meaningful, prosperous life that we desire.

Reflective Practice:

Part II is designed to help you let go of the fear of scarcity. Chapter 4 focuses on the integration between mind, body, and spirit and the importance of seeking ways to further develop your *spiritual and moral lines*. Both lines are key to how we make decisions and are therefore important to our experience of time and money.

Please review the descriptors for these two lines in Appendix D section of this book. Then, spend some time deciding upon one specific practice you might engage in over the next month to help you more fully experience movement in these two areas. For example, you might decide to focus on your spiritual development by engaging in prayer or meditation. Or, you might decide to pay closer attention to what values you rely on to make moral decisions with respect to time and money. At least once a week, journal your responses to the following questions:

- What is the spiritual or moral practice that you decided upon?
- How consistent have you been in this practice over the last month?
- What patterns are you seeing within yourself as a result of this practice?
- How has your spiritual or moral practice impacted your time/money decisions?

5

SCARCITY BELIEFS ABOUT MONEY

David was one of the brightest leaders I'd ever encountered. As a former client, colleague, and friend, I had high hopes for our working relationship within my own practice. Because this man had twenty-plus years of corporate experience, I knew I had to allow time for his adjustment into an entrepreneurial arrangement. I also knew that he had a history of stops and starts in his career, and while I did have some level of concern about the nature of those transitions, I felt his expertise was worth the effort.

After months, dare I admit years, of working with David to achieve financial results, I finally came to an important realization. It didn't matter how much time and energy I put into David. He simply was not able to produce even one new client for the business.

One afternoon, in desperation, I asked him a pointed question.

"What do you *believe* about people with money?"

His response was astonishing.

"I believe they're egocentric, greedy, and oppressive," he replied.

I remember silently thinking to myself, "Well, no wonder I can't get you to make any money." What I learned in that moment was actually the catapult for my curiosity about the belief systems people have tied to time and money. David's negative beliefs about people with money helped me begin to understand the attitudes and behaviors he had exhibited over our five-year relationship. Simply stated, David had consistently expressed a scarcity mindset of fear on many levels. There was never enough money to meet his financial responsibilities. He never felt valued for the work he did in previous roles. He had a history of financial failures. While he portended that he was not "driven by money," he was actually held hostage by the lack thereof. Further, he continued to place himself and his family in precarious financial situations. The scarcity perspectives that David endured blocked any ability to step into more abundant perspectives and greater success.

What I knew about David's early history was that he had come from an inner-city environment that supported his belief system. I failed to realize, however, that no matter how hard I tried, I did not have the power to change those beliefs. His beliefs had hardened into a cynical attitude toward people who had acquired success and wealth. He didn't yet know how to go about the hard work of making meaning out of those early experiences. Failure to do so had shackled him to a life of scarcity, fear, and self-sabotage.

Our beliefs dictate our actions, sometimes at a subconscious level. We self-sabotage and don't even know it. Years later, as I thought about my colleague's work and life history, the patterns were even more obvious. Even though David was extremely talented, he had a litany of repeated failures accompanied by a cycle of financial chaos.

If you're a business leader reading this example, you may have had similar experiences with an employee or colleague who just couldn't seem to produce results. No matter how hard you tried, you just couldn't help this person step into his full potential. It is a frustrating experience to witness someone with talent struggle in such ways.

Conflicting fears about money often lie at the heart of the gap between potential and actual results. Suffice to say that David's scenario was perhaps a bit more dramatic than most, but in my early discovery process, I came to realize that David is not much different than many of us. We all have a subconscious story about money. On some level, we may even know we need to make a change, but we simply don't know how.

As I've suggested, that first step in making change is always going to be awareness of your own story and how that story has impacted your dimensions of self. But, in order to make meaning from that new awareness, we must answer a preliminary question: Are my beliefs about money enhancing or ruining my life? It's an important question because the answer tells you if you are building a life of contentment and prosperity or a life based on fear.

What Are You Telling Yourself About Money?

Someone once said to me that attitude is the thing that walks through the door before we do. I like the visual of that premise. On any given day, I'd like to think that my positive attitude struts into the meeting room before I even arrive. But, what about those days when our bank account is overdrawn? If you have a history of money shortages, then it's not too difficult to imagine yourself embodying an attitude of scarcity. So, yes, we have a money attitude,[14] what some thought leaders postulate as a form of social intelligence that determines our motives, behaviors, and understanding of money.[15] In the sphere of money, our attitude can equate to fear and scarcity or an empowering sense of freedom and abundance.

Because of these tendencies, let's further explore the difference between abundance and scarcity and how these aspects of our belief systems can translate into either fear or freedom.

Abundance vs. Scarcity

Up to this point, I have intermittently directed our discussion to the cognitive, emotional, interpersonal, spiritual, and moral lines of development. I have also eluded to the multi-faceted "types" of human development which may include such things as personality, temperament, age, culture, upbringing, gender, and a host of other variables that come into play. Each of these dimensions adds to the complexity of the previously-described stages, lines, and states of human development, and they culminate into attitudes or a worldview about life to include our attitudes and beliefs about money. My research further suggests a continuum of thought patterns that encompass a range of perspectives from scarcity to abundance.

Before I describe the distinctions of these findings, let's first examine some basic definitions:

Abundance is a belief that

- there are *enough* resources for self and others;
- resources are part of an *ongoing cycle of renewal*;[16]
- I have the *ability to produce* what I need and want; and
- I am *worthy* of such resources.

This is abundance in its simplest form, and it represents a host of behaviors that result in greater creativity, a sense of freedom, a spirit of generosity, and higher levels of self-efficacy.

Scarcity is quite obviously the opposite. When we operate from a mindset of scarcity, there never seems to be enough, we believe ourselves unworthy of what is available, and our behaviors produce paralysis and an unwillingness to contribute.

Scarcity perspectives may also cause us to self-sabotage. When we operate from scarcity, we are essentially living from a perspective that there is not enough to go around. Scarcity produces uncertainty, confusion, and fear, and fear produces nothing but more scarcity.

Now, let's embark on a deeper exploration into how this sense of fear and scarcity shows up in our life when we're chasing time *and* money.

My Findings on the Experience of Time and Money

The nature of research is that we delineate one construct separate and apart from another and examine it closely, so it goes without saying that in my work, I had to explore money separate from time. Even so, one of my contentions, as you may recall, is that our experience of time and money are related. For example, to date, the results of my research indicate that people who have attitudes of scarcity or abundance with respect to money, also indicate similar attitudes with respect to time. Accordingly, several major themes have consistently emerged in relation to the continuum on money.[17] I have analyzed and broken down those themes into the following five categories[1]

1. *Outward Expressions*: thoughts, feelings, emotions, or perceptions about money.
2. *Self-Efficacy*: beliefs about one's ability to earn money or impact one's overall financial freedom.
3. *Financial Responsibility*: attitudes, beliefs, or behaviors associated with handling money in a proactive manner.

---

1   *Appendix A further delineates these details of the High-to-Moderate Money Scarcity storylines.

4. *Ability to Plan for the Future*: capacity to make financial choices in the present that will impact the potential for financial stability in the future.

5. *Potential for Generosity*: thoughts, feelings, or actions about sharing or giving to others; inability to give to others for fear of not having enough for one's own basic needs.

With Outward Expressions, for example, those individuals who scored in the High-to-Moderate Money Scarcity range indicated feelings of guilt, stress, helplessness, worry, or fear. Such emotional responses have the potential to result in shame, anxiety, frustration, or anger over money, or the lack thereof. Within this context, I observed two primary scarcity storylines that people may experience when it comes to money.[18]

High Money Scarcity Storyline #1: *I'll never have enough money.*
If you're someone who predominately lives from a High Money Scarcity perspective, it really doesn't matter how much money you make. In your worldview, you'll never have enough. People who fall within this range may have experienced poverty in their early-childhood years and, because of those early-childhood experiences, still fear that their financial resources will suddenly disappear.

However, poverty doesn't necessarily produce a mindset of scarcity. The amount of money you actually make does *not* determine your mindset. People who have substantial financial means can also have a mindset of high scarcity. For those who have wealth, for example, scarcity might show up as unhealthy competitiveness and greed. Remember, scarcity stems from a *belief* that you'll never have enough, even if the belief isn't necessarily accurate.

When I think of a keen example of scarcity, I think of Jordan Belfort. You might remember *The Wolf of Wall Street* wherein Leonardo

DiCaprio portrayed Belfort at the height of his Wall Street mania.[19] How much is fact or fiction, we'll probably never know, but the fact remains that Belfort squandered millions of dollars on sex, drugs, expensive cars, houses, and women. As the movie portrays, it didn't matter how much money he had or how many toys he acquired, there was never enough. The hungry beast of *more* always needed to be fed, and this beast of scarcity eventually led to his self-destruction.

For most of us, scarcity rears its ugly head in far less destructive ways, but it always produces some level of fear. Stand in fear often and long enough, and you become paralyzed. We're no longer chasing money; money is now chasing us. We stand frozen, unable to exercise choice. And, when we feel outside choice, life becomes an endless cycle of more, more, and more. There is never enough to quench the hunger. For some of us, that hungry beast transforms into very specific, self-destructive pathologies associated with money.

If we want to pursue money in healthier ways, we have to face the beast within. Let's now explore the two key perspectives that have emerged in conjunction with High Money Scarcity Storyline #1 as a way to help you reevaluate your own personal and professional perspectives on money.

Perspective No. 1: The Compensation See-Saw
Our sense of scarcity can often play out in how we ask for and receive just compensation for the work that we do. Scarcity can show up in surprising ways. For example, certain individuals may want unrealistic compensation for what they do whereas others may ask for too little or perhaps nothing at all. In the marketplace, this often plays out in what I call a "Compensation See-Saw." When exploring this potential, it's useful to consider whether you are being justly compensated for the value you're providing.

People in the "too little compensation" category are often highly responsible individuals. They get up each day, go to work, and do their best, but they just can't seem to get ahead. Sometimes their inability to earn higher compensation translates into a sense of not being enough. They come to believe that they're not smart enough, good enough, or high enough on the food chain to earn a healthy living. Additionally, people in this subcategory may have a tendency to give their time away (via volunteer efforts) or to work for very low-paying wages. Hiding out in low-paying jobs or worthy causes is sometimes a way to erase emotions of guilt or shame over not being able to ask for just compensation.

This is not to say that there isn't a time and season for volunteerism. Volunteer work is a meaningful experience that can enhance a sense of abundance, but it should be balanced with an ability to earn (unless, of course, you're retired). The lesson here is that it's important to balance the effort of hard work, volunteer or otherwise, with the need for just compensation.

Perspective No. 2: Inappropriate Money Talk
In this subcategory, people tend to either avoid conversations about money or talk about money all the time. Both perspectives point to some level of financial insecurity. Try spending just two days listening to your internal and external chatter about money and note what you observe. If you have fear-based conversations running in your mind, you'll notice one of two things: You're either an *Avoider*, eluding any and all conversations related to money with your family, friends, colleagues, and employees, or you're an *Annoyer*, talking about money all the time to anyone who will listen. Many of us know several people who fall into one of these categories. Unfortunately, neither of these approaches is serving your capacity to shift into a more abundant lifestyle.

If You're an Avoider...

There may be serious issues that need to be addressed, but there is also an opportunity to experience a far less stressful relationship with money by doing the work required to shift your perspective. Try sitting in a quiet space and thinking about what money issues you're avoiding. Are you making too little to cover your expenses? Is your spouse spending too much? Are you afraid that a budget will restrict you from enjoying life?

When we're in the middle of life transitions, it may seem easier to avoid the hard money conversations until we're actually in crisis. Addressing these issues before they become a crisis will eliminate a lot of negative emotions about money. The bigger payoff is that you'll start to experience more positive results.

Whatever the source of your avoidance, write it down and then begin to think of ways to overcome those issues.

If You're an Annoyer...

There's nothing worse than being out with someone who is constantly chattering about the cost of every little thing you do. I find that most people don't even realize they're engaging in inappropriate money talk. It's a habit. This behavior can be an indicator that there's a lack of controlled spending. Every purchased item is a surprise attack.

Pay attention to what you say about money because what you say reflects what you think and what you believe. This is particularly important if you have children. Causing them to worry about every dime they spend is not the same thing as teaching them how to manage money. People who plan, prepare, and manage their money don't have to talk about it all the time. Money is a tool, and they know how to use it—no matter how much or little they have.

Appendix A points to several other significant storylines that may arise in High Money Scarcity to include the inability to engage with finances in responsible ways or to plan for the future. When we live from such perspectives of scarcity, it can be challenging to think and act beyond our own survival. Additionally, our potential for generosity is greatly affected because we fear that if we contribute our financial resources to others, we may not have enough left over to meet our basic needs.

Remember, your words are a window into your belief systems, even your character, and they are also a source of power—which brings me to the second money storyline.

Moderate Money Scarcity Storyline #2:
I must work hard to earn and be responsible.

This second primary scarcity storyline is perhaps the most detrimental because when we work hard and act in responsible ways, we can deceive ourselves into believing that we're living in the freedom of abundance. You may be driven by responsibility, and this can either be a good or bad thing—all depending on how you balance perspectives on scarcity and abundance. If you want to know if it's freedom or fear that's driving your responsible self, just notice the emotions and behaviors that rise up out of your so-called "responsibility." Negative emotions, such as guilt, fear, or shame, can be clear indicators that scarcity thinking is holding you captive. Are you enjoying life or worried and angry all the time? Our sense of responsibility is another beast that can hold us hostage and produce the fear of scarcity.

While the behaviors associated with this second storyline are less destructive and perhaps less obvious than the first storyline, there is still a significant opportunity to reduce money-related stress, and by doing so, to increase your enjoyment of life. People who struggle with this storyline may believe that money makes the world go round, but they may also believe that if they *just work hard enough*, they will change their financial situation. It's not what they do in terms of hard work that's the issue here. It's the intention behind what they do because, once again, the question is whether any amount of hard work will ever be enough.

The good news is that such individuals may understand that they have some level of control over the money they earn and how they spend it. This is a huge shift in the right direction particularly if they were once someone who believed they had no control at all over their capacity to earn and spend. Remember, we are all works-in-progress. This is all about human development, and even the "destination" of freedom and abundance is a place of continuous growth. Patience is required when we're attempting to move from scarcity to abundance.

As with the first High Money Scarcity storyline, several major perspectives surfaced that can affect people's personal and professional lives.

Perspective No. 1: The Yoke of Responsibility
In this perspective, people may fall into the trap of believing that they carry the burden of financial responsibility all by themselves. Life itself may not feel like much fun; it is, in fact, burdensome. The yoke of responsibility is a heavy cross to bear. If you fall into this subcategory, you may be balancing this sense of responsibility well. However, you may also be riddled by your sense of obligation such that you may not have much time to enjoy the trip along the way.

For example, you may have a tendency to budget, save, and prioritize your money, however, you might go overboard in this regard out of fear of not having enough. When I think of this propensity to go overboard, I'm reminded of clients I've encountered who complain about missing out on things they want to do or have. By this I mean, they are so busy budgeting, saving, and prioritizing, they miss the joy of life. Vacations are for someone else because maybe they're stockpiling money for retirement. Or, maybe, they fail to include their spouse in hard financial choices because they think they need to carry the burden alone. Remember, a budget is useful in keeping you on track, but it should include some level of flexibility so that you don't shift into high levels of stress or anxiety when emergencies arise.

You may feel like you're being responsible when in reality, you're making fear-based decisions. For those who slip into this perspective, it can also be helpful to notice if you avoid calculated risks or new opportunities. If you're someone who tends to take the safer route to success or monetary gain, be sure to examine your motives behind those decisions.

Responsibility, then, may equate to good enough earnings, but life is still safe, and you may operate from fear and a sense of not having enough. You may have been taught to be grateful for the work you have, not to waste money on frivolous things—and pretty much everything outside your basic needs is considered frivolous.

People who have childhood stories about the value and importance of a high work ethic often come from this perspective. A high work ethic is vital to success as long as you are:

- fulfilling your purpose and at least moving toward some work you enjoy;
- being justly compensated for that work;
- not making fear-based decisions regarding what you save and how you invest; and
- being intentional about the trip along the way.

Perspective No. 2: Money as Static
This second perspective refers to people who may not yet understand when to hold 'em and when to fold 'em. In this scenario, people believe that money requires effort, so they may have a greater tendency to want to hold on to what they acquire. When we work to hold on to what we have, we can become prisoners to our belongings.

Understanding the flow of money is essential to our having a healthier experience with money. This means we must face the reality that money comes and goes. Sometimes we have more money than other times. For example, you may have a business or real estate investment that is depreciating. It may be time to let go of investments or sell off certain things that you originally viewed as important to your sense of financial security. What toys are you holding on to?

This is one perspective that I personally struggle with every time my husband and I have to make hard choices. I reflect on the significance of the recession in 2008. My husband is in real estate and land development. We enjoyed the building boom of the 80s and had the toys to prove it. But, when the recession hit in 2008, we had to make some choices. I was brought up to believe that you hold on tightly to whatever stuff you acquire. In my worldview, that stuff represents safety, security, and resources for retirement in later years. So, you can imagine my discomfort when my husband came home one day and said that he thought it best to put some property we owned on the market.

To me, this direction equated to failure and a loss of safety and future security. After all, people everywhere were losing their homes and their jobs. "Are we next?" I wondered. To him, this decision was simply a business decision based on changes in the market. What the numbers told him was that property taxes were going to rise even as the property itself was about to depreciate—both factors representing a significant loss. I had trouble letting go, but in the end, I came to understand that my husband's success is, in part, due to his understanding of the flow of money.

Remember our abstract conversation on money? Money is not constant; it fluctuates. People who live in abundance, and beyond the threat of scarcity, understand this flow.

Understanding the flow of money dictates also that we never get too attached to our possessions. This premise can be particularly challenging when you hold a worldview, as I did, that holding on to what you acquire is a sign of being responsible. Acquisitions and personal possessions are resources. It is wise to understand that, like a flowing river, those resources shift and change. Whereas I would prefer holding on to our investments out of fear and scarcity, my husband views our possessions as resources available to help us weather unexpected storms.

Perspective No. 3: The Dark Side of Generosity
Not all giving is created equal. A mindset of scarcity breeds a different type of generosity. Those with this perspective may experience extreme emotions when it comes to how they express generosity. Some, for example might give from an unhealthy sense of obligation whereas others may equate their own self-worth to how much they give.

Generosity, as a virtue, is a slippery slope as it has its own spectrum of nuances. I'll dive into the essence of authentic generosity in a later chapter. For now, let's discuss this moderate scarcity perspective as Forced Generosity, a tendency to give from the wallet rather than from a generous heart. For instance, you might contribute to various charities, tithe at your local church, or even feed the homeless, but are you giving out of obligation or are you giving from a generous heart that truly cares?

There is a difference.

If you're giving from obligation, you're most likely experiencing a lot of negative emotions. Stress, worry, anxiety, or even resentment may be closely linked to your giving. You may find it difficult to be joyful about giving. You may live in fear that giving to others will drain your own resources such that you're unable to meet your family responsibilities. This deep and abiding sense of responsibility is a step beyond the fear of generosity as indicated in the High Money Scarcity category, but it is fear-based just the same. People in the moderate category do not necessarily engage in bouts of egocentric spending that hinders their ability to share or contribute to others. Such acts would be considered irresponsible. Even so, they may only give when they have a surplus, and when is there ever a surplus?

One extreme example of Moderate Money Scarcity is narcissistic generosity. I like to think of this type of generosity as one of the "imposters of abundance." Here's what I mean.

Researchers Rosenthal and Pittinsky define pathological narcissism to include traits of grandiosity, arrogance, self-absorption, entitlement, fragile self-esteem, and hostility.[20] The narcissist, in her quest for power, is the poster child for Moderate Money Scarcity because, while there may be enough financial resources, the underlying reason for giving is cloaked in a need for more and more recognition, love, sex, position, or status.

For the narcissist, moderate scarcity may prove even more complex because regardless of financial status, the narcissist gives whether or not she has money. This type of generosity is an "imposter" because while it may appear self-sacrificing, it actually stems from a depraved sense of self. In extreme cases, this type of individual may be addicted to giving, even willing to go into debt. The giving, you see, is more about looking good than it is authentic generosity.

One of my favorite Netflix series *The Tutors* offers up a great illustration of narcissistic generosity.[21] The work explores the life and wives of Henry VIII in a very engaging way. As I moved through the series, I was struck by the opulence of Henry's reign and his portrayal of narcissistic generosity.

By all historical (and fictional) accounts, King Henry VIII was a man of excess. Lust and gluttony ruled his life. He gave opulent jewels to the women he treasured—gifts just as easily rescinded when he'd decide to tumble into bed with his next conquest. Off with her head, as the saying goes, with no apparent guilt or remorse.

While we're not privy to the inner workings of Henry's mind, what we do know is that he engaged in god-like behaviors that ultimately positioned his egocentric desires above and beyond the church itself. History tells us that the church was, at that time, plagued by its own narcissistic leaders, so maybe this wasn't such a bad thing. If the series resembles history in even the slightest way, what we witness is a man who believed he was beyond the laws of nature and the laws of God.

Such is the path of the narcissist. From this pathology, the narcissist gives to others, but beware! There are always strings attached because the narcissistic giver believes it's her right to give and take away at will. The rules of good conduct do not apply to the narcissist. What history witnessed in King Henry VIII was an unraveling of mind, body, and spirit—devastation of the highest order manifested in a man out of control of his life and his kingdom. Even moderate scarcity can breed depravity, and that hole can never be filled with anything but love. Six wives later, as the story goes, and Henry was never able to fill that hole.

These two money storylines and the perspectives associated with them represent High-to-Moderate Money Scarcity perspectives that can catapult us into survivor mode. The emotions associated with survival mode are pretty intense. Pay attention to any rising outward expressions of guilt, stress, helplessness, worry, or fear. More importantly, is the intensity of these emotions sometimes resulting in shame, anxiety, frustration, or even anger?

If you're living from paycheck to paycheck, you probably have good reason to be in survival mode. You're more than likely worried and fearful much of the time. Scarce amounts of money quickly turn into "scared money." If you're playing with scared money, you can't thrive, you can't create, and you won't be able to draw opportunity toward you. But, please don't despair. There are ways to move beyond perspectives of High-to-Moderate Money Scarcity.

Reflective Practice:

Chapter 5 addresses High-to-Moderate Scarcity beliefs about money. This reflective practice will focus on your sense of *responsibility* with respect to money. Go back into your early childhood memories and think about some of the messages you received from your parents or family about being "financially responsible." For example, if your parents worked at the same jobs for thirty years and lived in the same two-bedroom house throughout their 45 years of marriage, you may have been taught that it's irresponsible to explore new job opportunities or that it's wasteful to move into a larger home. Pick one significant story that you can remember. Based on that significant memory, spend 15-20 minutes journaling your responses to the following questions:

- What were some of the significant messages you received, or didn't receive, about being financially responsible?
- How do those messages impact your experience of money today?
- What patterns of responsibility are keeping you from experiencing a more meaningful experience of life?

6

SCARCITY BELIEFS ABOUT TIME

I f you're like many of us in today's ever-crazy world, you're probably feeling like you're being stalked by the clock. There just aren't enough hours in the day. We've already discussed how both the abstract and concrete aspects of time can compound our feelings of confusion, frustration, and anxiety, all of which add to our sense of being stressed and overwhelmed.[2] One of the reasons we so readily slip into a mindset of time scarcity is that we live in a consumer world designed to make us believe that we need more and more just to keep up.[22] If your experience of time is cloaked in any of these expressions of self on a regular basis, there's a good chance that you're running on

---

2   Scarcity marketing is turning us into scarcity robots. We are inundated with commercials, FaceBook ads, emails, and online courses that demand that we act now, know more immediately, grab that sale, buy the latest app, engage in the most recent platforms—and, if we don't, the world will pass us by. The faster we run, the harder we work, the less time we seem to have.

empty. There's an equally good chance that your experience of time is based on the scarcity perspectives that we've been discussing.

Before we can move away from that scarcity mindset and master an abundant perspective on time, we first have to acknowledge, head-on, what scarcity of time looks like and how it might be manifested in our own lives.

Similar to my research on money, several major storylines emerged in relation to High-to-Moderate Time Scarcity perspectives.[3] With respect to time, I analyzed and broke down the themes into the following five categories:

1. *Outward Expressions*: the thoughts, feelings, emotions, or perceptions about time.
2. *Self-efficacy*: beliefs and/or actions related to one's ability to manage time.
3. *Experience of Time*: how one experiences time based on perceptions or worldview.
4. *Sense of Accomplishment*: how one experiences a sense of completion at the end of each day/week/year.
5. *Potential for Generosity*: perspective on sharing or giving of one's time to others.

With regard to Outward Expressions, for example, having scarcity storylines about time may lead to feelings of constraint, frustration, a sense of being overwhelmed or chased by the clock, guilt, and shame at not being productive enough, and a belief that you have no control over your day. Within this context, I observed two primary High-to-Moderate Scarcity storylines that people may experience when it comes to time.

---

3   Appendix B further delineates these details of High-to-Moderate Time Scarcity storylines.

High Time Scarcity Storyline #1:
I never have enough time to get it all done.
People who experience this storyline are those most radically impacted by that ticking clock. We've all felt this at one time or another, but if you're consistently stressed about how little time you have, or if you're finding yourself working long and ridiculous hours just to keep up, it's possible that you feel as though you are being stalked by the clock.

You may have been taught, at an early age, the importance of staying busy. From your perspective, "Idleness is the devil's workshop." Good use of time means being productive, and if you're not utilizing every moment of your day, you may experience guilt.

Your sense of being chased by the clock may also cause you to feel as though time passes too quickly. If you're constantly busy, but your busyness is not attached to fulfilling and meaningful outcomes, you may feel that life itself is quickly passing you by and that you have no control over your time, your day, or even your life. Everything seems like a priority, and you just can't get to the things that you'd like to do; you may have great difficulty even scheduling priorities.

A high need for productivity may also cause you to flip between procrastination and a "do it now" mentality. When you experience yourself as running against time over extended periods, you may have a tendency to simply shut down and move to a place of inertia. You choose instead to do nothing. This could be a good thing if it allows you ample time to recover from stressful moments. The main issue is that you may have difficulty giving yourself permission for this choice. What happens instead is that you take time for yourself, but in doing so, you experience guilt and shame.

Within this High Time Scarcity storyline, let's examine three key perspectives people tend to have that are showing up in my research and how they negatively impact people's experience of time in their professional or personal lives

Perspective No. 1: Everything is a Priority

When everything is a priority, nothing is a priority. People who live with this perspective believe they have to get *everything* done, and they have to get it all done now!

With a high scarcity mindset, daily activities can easily become muddled and confusing. In other words, you have no real plan of action on how to best utilize your time. This lack of planning creates a cycle of stress that causes people with this perspective to believe everything is a priority—all of the time. It's not too difficult to understand how this cycle results in fear.

Such individuals often find themselves jumping from task to task in the hopes of getting more done when, in reality, a lack of focus keeps them from accomplishing much at all. The result? At the end of the day, they are often depleted of energy and left with a sense that the day has been wasted. Time marches on, and with each passing day, they become more frustrated and overwhelmed.

Scarcity of time demands that we work harder to accomplish more, and when this doesn't happen, we eventually wear out and shut down. Our inability to prioritize also causes us to slip into procrastination or inertia and feelings of guilt and shame.

Sometimes life dictates that we have a great many priorities. Sometimes we create "fire drill" priorities to fulfill our need for urgency and even chaos. One way that we do this is by procrastinating on deadlines, killing ourselves to meet them, and then celebrating that "we got through" the day, activity, or event. This may sound odd and curious but a perspective that associates personal value with productivity can cause us to slip into addictive uses, or misuses, of time.

This brings us to another perspective people tend to have about time that can negatively impact their personal or professional lives

Perspective No. 2: Urgency Addiction

People who operate from this perspective live from a self-defeating mantra: *I procrastinate because I do my best work when I'm under fire.*

In the early 80s, the acclaimed author Stephen Covey coined the phrase "urgency addict." With this phrase came a greater understanding of our propensity to misuse time and to create urgency and chaos in our lives. If you're an urgency addict, you probably put off priorities until they reach the point of crisis—until they become urgent. In his famous model, Covey offers the distinction between living from a place of urgency and living from a place where we truly learn to prioritize the most important aspects of life.[23]

Allow me to make a confession right now. I'm a reformed urgency addict. Covey's work changed my experience of time. As I developed awareness about my addiction to urgency and need to feel busy, I learned to think about and respond to time better. Remember, the difference between freedom and fear is about our perceptions of time and money. I'm still equally busy, I just think about my use of time in far more balanced and realistic ways.

This sounds easy enough, but for the urgency addict, there's a payoff that must be overcome. The payoff is this: As an urgency addict, you get to feel extremely busy, productive, and important. The adrenaline rush associated with all of this, however, often equates to extreme levels of stress and anxiety that are less than healthy.

Just like any other addiction, urgency addiction creates stress for the people around us. You might find yourself in constant conflict with people you care about. For example, I used to literally believe that I could move time. I'd take on way too many projects with little to no awareness as to how all those projects impacted my team, and, worse yet, my family. What I failed to recognize was that my team was often left behind to implement the details of my latest brainchild as I moved on to the next one. The result? I positioned them to feel chased by the same clock that was chasing me. The only problem was they weren't urgency addicts. I was. To add insult to injury, I wasn't always as generous with my time. Too often, my urgency addiction pushed me to places where I totally disrespected my team's time.

If you feel like you're moving through the world with your hair on fire most of the day, you'll have to do some work on moving past urgency addiction. People who fall into this category often have professions that require them to respond to stressful situations in the moment. It's the kind of stressful environment one might encounter in a hospital emergency room setting. Most of us, however, are not in the daily trenches of life-threatening situations. We just behave as if we are. The question is—are you creating unnecessary levels of stress for yourself or others due to an urgency addiction?

There are dozens of reasons that we adopt the perspective of an urgency addict. The point is to become more aware of when this is happening and to adopt better practices so that you can be more proactive.

Perspective No. 3: A Lone-Ranger Mentality

The Lone Ranger has a deep-seated need for control. This person believes that it will take more time to train or delegate the task at hand, so he might as well do it himself. This need for control might even spill over into difficulty working in a team environment.

This perspective circles back to everything being a priority. If everything is a priority, you're running as fast as you can each day. It may seem easier for you to complete the task yourself than to take the time to delegate or train someone else. It will be important to recognize when you're trying to go it alone. Delegation is a difficult process for someone who lives from scarcity because of the perception that it's easier and faster to do it yourself.

If you find yourself feeling as though you've accomplished little or nothing at the end of each day—no matter how many mountains you've climbed—it may be time to ask yourself if you're living from a Lone-Ranger mentality. While this level of time scarcity may mislead you into feeling like a hero, ultimately, you're self-sabotaging your success.

This perspective points to yet another significant question: How might the failure to delegate cause undue stress for others? The Lone Ranger may exhibit many of the same behaviors as an urgency addict, the only difference being that in the failure to delegate, he also fails to empower those around him. People who live and work with a Lone Ranger often feel controlled, underappreciated, and unable to successfully fulfill their roles and responsibilities.

To reiterate, Appendix B points to an inadequate sense of self-efficacy with respect to time to include a poor to almost non-existent sense of accomplishment at the end of the day. Additionally, people who fall into this category may exercise a Lack of Generosity when it comes to their use of time in relation to others. Any potential to procrastinate or disregard other people's time may result in ongoing and consistent conflict with others.

Moderate Time Scarcity Storyline #2:
I must be productive and exercise efficient use of time.
People who experience this storyline view time through the lens of efficiency and productivity. Productivity is a good thing as long as the intention behind this perspective is balanced. A challenge arises, however, if you find it difficult to allow quality time for family and friends. Another challenge arises if you're finding that even when you do make time for family and recreation, it may not be as consistent as you'd like. If you're one who falls into this, such inconsistency may be causing undue stress, guilt, or anxiety.

Remember, we've been making the distinction between the concrete and abstract experience of time. People who live from this storyline, often experience time in concrete ways. They may be extremely conscientious about making appointments on time, but if work is placed before recreation and family, they may find it difficult to be fully present in the moment. They may feel as though they are slaves to their calendars and feel guilty wherever they are.

Within the Moderate Time Scarcity storyline, I observed three key perspectives that tend to keep people from moving into a more abundant experience of time. These perspectives are not necessarily bad in and of themselves. However, when experienced to an out-of-balance extreme, negative emotions and undue stress often surface.

Perspective No. 1: Time is Money

People with a perspective of "time is money" may have trouble taking time for leisure activities or anything that is not producing direct income. Time is not to be wasted but accounted for by earnings. The mantra here is: *I feel stressed when I'm at work and guilty when I'm recreating at home.* If this is your worldview, you may find it difficult to balance work with family, recreation, and your own self-care. You may have trouble giving yourself permission to enjoy other aspects of life beyond work. Stress and guilt become part of the equation because whether you're at work or at home, you always feel as though you should have done more at the "other place." Without attention to consistent balance, you risk becoming a workaholic.

Again, this is a tricky perspective to acknowledge within ourselves because it is clouded in responsible behavior. One way to determine if this type of thinking is sabotaging your life is to pay attention to the remarks of your spouse, significant other, children, or friends. If you're hearing significant complaints about your lack of attention to their needs, it might be a good sign that you're leaning in this direction.

Perspective No. 2: Time Must be "Managed."
This perspective aligns even more closely with the responsible side of who we are. The mantra? A person who falls within this perspective will proudly tell you: *I live by my calendar. I am a master at time management.*

I can remember being quite proud of my Franklin Day timer and how well I organized my time. I prided myself on having every meeting, action, and task closely tallied and monitored via my calendar. I loved being a busy person and being able to account for every hour of my day. The problem was, I wasn't managing my calendar. My calendar was managing me. If something unexpected came up—and, it often did—I was quickly overwhelmed. There was simply no room on the calendar for unforeseen moments.

If you're like I was, you probably enjoy having a time management system that keeps you on track. This system, however, will cause you undue stress and frustration if it's too rigid. Here again, a desire to rigidly manage time comes from a concrete experience of time. A rigid time management system, in whatever form, fails to include a lot of white space on the calendar so that you can freely respond to people, events, and situations that come up unexpectedly.

How do you know if you fall into this perspective?

Here's a quick checkpoint that might help. Notice if you're feeling like you didn't get anything done at the end of the day and you're going to bed stressed and overwhelmed. If so, you may be allowing your time management system to run your life. Or, if you're waking in the middle of the night with a do-to list on your mind, remember, a time management system is there to help you be more productive. Being productive includes being free of any negative emotions about time. If you're not experiencing some level of freedom—if negative emotions are clouding your ability to experience successful outcomes—it may be time to rethink how you're scheduling your time.

Perspective No. 3: Time Must be "Balanced."

This next perspective is subtly aligned with the first two. The difference is that the conflict lies within a conscious desire for something more.

People with this perspective indicate a desire for work/life balance but lack the knowledge or skills on how to get there. Within this perspective, I am seeing people who believe that their love for family is competing with their need to earn. The giving of one's time, then, equates to Sporadic Generosity as depicted in Appendix B. This separation between desire and reality also results in the same negative emotions we've seen repeatedly come up: guilt, shame, and a sense of being overburdened.

This perspective stems from a belief that the most important thing a person can do is to provide for family needs. The question is, are you physically and mentally absent in the process? If so, you may find yourself strongly connected with the "time is money" conversation. Of course, being a good provider is a noble, responsible act. What's missing here is the capacity to turn a desire for life balance into reality. People with this worldview often have trouble recognizing their responsibility to their own health and to being fully present with those they care about. Giving of one's time is valued in relation to honoring time commitments and being on time. Such a worldview doesn't always allow for the desired life balance because, in essence, time with loved ones is too often more task-oriented than it is relational.

If, for example, I'm merely stopping by my son's little league game on the way to an appointment, I might feel like a responsible parent in that, in the midst of my busy day, I got to the game in the first place. I honored my commitment. I can check this task off my list. This, however, is a very different experience for you and your son than one that encompasses a time commitment of being present and fully engaged for the entire game.

Clearly, we can't be all things to all people all of the time. The point is to examine what you're thinking, the intention behind that thought, and the actions and outcomes as a result of that thinking. Are you living from moderate scarcity? Remember, we tend to move in and out of these various perspectives depending on what's going on in our lives. If you're seeing a glimpse of yourself in the perspectives associated with Time Scarcity Storyline No.1, which represents higher levels of scarcity, there is considerable retooling of your thought patterns and behaviors that may need to occur.

If, on the other hand, you're seeing yourself in the perspectives associated with Time Scarcity Storyline No. 2, which represents a more moderate level of scarcity, you're perfectly positioned to move into a more abundant experience of time that will change your life. Paying close attention to the Reflective Practice recommendations at the end of this chapter is a useful first step to begin that process.

To recap, my work has identified two major "scarcity" storylines for time and money that have the potential to hold people back from experiencing more meaningful and prosperous lives. The first storylines of each are more fear based. The second storylines of each are more grounded in responsible beliefs and behaviors, but these perspectives have not yet fully emerged into thoughts and actions associated with abundance. Irrespective of whether the scarcity mindset is based in fear or a heightened sense of responsibility, however, it's still scarcity, and the result is often the same: a cycle of struggle that ultimately prevents people from experiencing greater fulfillment in their lives. While moderate levels of scarcity suggest that you're on your way toward more abundant perspectives, there's still considerable work to be done. The additional challenge is that moderate levels of scarcity can easily fool us into believing that our behaviors stem from a level of efficiency and responsibility.

Reflective Practice

Chapter 6 addresses High-to-Moderate Scarcity beliefs about time. The practice prescribed for this chapter focuses on *intentionality*. Select at least one of the perspectives that fall under the scarcity storylines of time. For example, you might want to focus on the perspective, "Time Must Be Managed" under the Moderate Time Scarcity Storyline No. 2 if that particular storyline resonates with your experience of time.

Based on the content in this chapter, determine a more abundant perspective for that storyline. You might decide to schedule recurring recreational time with a friend or family member. Or you might look at other ways to rid yourself of a rigid time management system. Once you've determined the storyline and perspective you want to focus on, spend 10-15 minutes each day, over the next seven days, journaling your responses to the following questions each evening:

- Which storyline did you select as most relevant to your experience of time right now?
- What specifically did you focus on to help you transform this storyline from one of scarcity to one of abundance?
- What thoughts or behaviors shifted as a result of this focus?
- What new action will you commit to moving forward as a result of this shift?

Part III

THE OPPORTUNITY:
STEPPING INTO
YOUR BIGGEST LIFE

7

BE THE DIRECTOR OF
YOUR OWN MOVIE

The 6-pound, 11-ounce baby boy was born at 6:01 am on an April Friday.

"Something is wrong with the baby" were the first words the young mother and father heard, words that would smack them both sideways. There was no way to prepare for such news. No way to make sense of what they were hearing. The newborn was immediately rushed into the Neonatal Intensive Care Unit, and while the other mothers nursed and held their babies through the night and into the next day, this young mother sat numb, alone in her hospital room, trying to make sense of the madness.

Just twenty-four hours previously, she had been overwhelmed with excitement at the thought of her soon-to-arrive baby. Her biggest worry? That her young toddler might someday stain the white carpet in their living room. Silently, her mind relived those intertwined moments of anticipated joy. They had responsibly waited to have their first child. Waited until the

73

house, the car, the savings, the careers were all well established. Waited so that their young son would have the promise of a better future.

What had gone wrong? How was it that they had come to be so unprepared?

The following morning, a doctor entered her hospital room and time stood still. She saw that the doctor's lips were moving, but she couldn't make sense of what he was saying. Something about surgery, the baby's heart, and a two-year lifespan?

The garbled words exploded inside her head; the train wreck of time, soft and loud all at once. Life, as she knew it, had forever changed.

Later that afternoon, the young mother entered NICU to watch her baby sleep beneath the plexiglass dome. "Maybe they'll let me hold him for a few moments," she thought to herself. The room was alive with beeping monitors and nurses busily attending to the newest arrivals. And, there in the midst of it all, she noticed a large sign, up, over, and to the right of the nurses' station. She stared in disbelief.

The sign read, "Thirty days to bankruptcy."

"That can't be right," she thought. "What does it mean?"

Later that evening, she expressed her fears to her husband. "Will we lose our home in thirty days if Michael's in NICU that long?"

"I don't know," he answered. "We have insurance. I just don't know. Whatever our son needs, we'll make sure he has it. If we have to sell everything, he'll get the best care. I promise."

Suddenly, the possibility of a stained carpet was the least of their worries. She could tell by the look on her husband's face that he was scared senseless. The previous day, they had been a carefree young couple who lived a life of abundance and joy. Today, with a newborn baby in NICU, the young couple was threatened by the beast of fear and scarcity. Its fangs penetrated the very soul of who they were. The grip so tight, she could barely breathe. There was no escape. They were trapped by the circumstances of their newly exploded life.

— — —

By now, you may have guessed that I was that young mother. My husband and I never did figure out what that bankruptcy sign meant. I suspect that it was something entirely different than what our imagination led us to believe. Even so, the reality of our newfound responsibilities hit us hard. Over the course of time, we would learn that our beautiful Michael had a rare metabolic disorder known as Cytochrome C Oxidase Deficiency. It would take years to unravel the fear and stress associated with having a child with special needs. Time and money would hold us hostage for at least two decades.

As it turned out, those early doctors were wrong. Even though Michael was physically disabled, he lived an amazing life until the age of twenty-seven. Still, those early years of fear and scarcity never left us. There never seemed to be enough time to meet Michael's many needs. Stress and worry consumed us. Would our health insurance be cancelled? Would we have enough money for yet another wheelchair or that much needed handicapped accessible van? And, as the end of Michael's life came crashing down upon us, as time began to run out and the hospital bills mounted, even then, all those many years later, I would find myself intermittently paralyzed by fear and scarcity.

So, it goes. Every person, every family, has their own past and present story. Life happens, and when we're thrown into uncharted territory, when the train wrecks and the ride comes to a sudden halt, time and money are almost always part of the equation.

The point is that life will always get in the way of our best laid plans. Things rarely turn out exactly as we'd hoped. By the simplest definition, life is a series of circumstances, and we sometimes don't have control over those circumstances. The good news is that we do have control over how we *think* about them. When we can make sense out of our circumstances in positive ways, we mature and grow. When we choose to fall victim to our circumstances in negative ways, we become stagnant, victims paralyzed by fear, and we may eventually even lose our sense of self.

One way that we can begin to make sense or "meaning" out of our circumstances is to develop the self-reflective capacity to witness our own thoughts in the moment. This self-reflective capacity helps us gain perspective so that we can exercise choice If you think of your life as a movie, the ability to witness allows you to switch from being the actor, who, within the confines of what he is told by directors and producers, has some influence over the portrayal of his character. You now get to be the director.

Here's what I mean.

Up to this point, we've considered several possibilities with respect to how each of us may experience time and money: 1) our early-childhood stories may be linked to our everyday experience of time and money; 2) time and money are paradoxical in nature; 3) our stories may equate to perspectives associated with either scarcity or abundance; and 4) a worldview of scarcity often equates to a fear-based experience of time and money.

If we are to successfully maneuver our way through the many complexities associated with time and money, greater self-awareness is required. When we step into greater awareness, we increase our capacity to influence our internal storylines in positive ways. We increase our potential to change.

Simply stated, what separates you from your dog Spot is that you have the potential to make meaning from your life experiences. It's how we grow, develop, and hopefully mature into responsible adults and progress through the stages of human development. When we learn to examine our own thinking in relation to the circumstances of our lives, we develop the practice of greater self-awareness. Over time, this practice grants us opportunity to experience behaviors associated with a more meaningful and fulfilling life. The best news of all is that you get to choose if that meaning is positive or negative—no matter your circumstances. It's the old adage come to life: Is the glass half empty or half full? You get to decide.

In those first weeks and months after Michael's birth, I wasn't able to make sense of anything. We were in survival mode doing all we could to get through each day. Over the course of many years, as our circumstances changed, there would be many opportunities for me to reflect on what was happening and how to make sense of it all. Time and money didn't always rule my thoughts and actions, but those two resources were always in the mix as we struggled with daily care, school systems, countless hospital visits, surgeries, exploratory tests, a multitude of doctors, insurance issues, the cost of therapies, wheelchairs, the need for transportation, home modifications, and on the list goes.

Did I live in scarcity and fear from the time my baby was born? Absolutely. For at least the first three years. Then, one day I made a conscious choice to slay that beast. I remember standing outside Michael's doorway listening for his breathing. As my hand lay frozen on the doorknob, I wondered, once again, "Will I walk through this door only to find him lifeless?" And, on that day, I made a decision to be the director of my own movie. I decided to pay close attention to my own thoughts and behaviors in relation to every situation and to closely examine the choices I made. Were my choices negative or positive? Did they benefit my son, or was I holding Michael hostage to my own fear?

I didn't always get it right. Sometimes the beast won, but I vowed to keep trying. I vowed that we would no longer live in fear. We wouldn't focus on the doctors' prediction of a two-year life span or how much money was needed to keep Michael alive. We would focus on quality of life. I adopted a mantra: *Sometimes you have to accept what is before you can do anything about what isn't.* What I didn't realize then was this mantra helped me utilize my resources of time and money differently. Rather than spending endless hours trying to find a cure, I learned to focus on strengthening Michael's abilities. For example, while there was no sense in spending money on a three-wheel bicycle he couldn't ride, a four-wheel electric fire engine was the perfect choice.

This change in perspective allowed me to move out of fear and scarcity and into the freedom of abundance. I focused on what we, as a family, had going for us, and I began to pay closer and closer attention to my own thoughts and behaviors. As I began to make different choices about how we would live out our daily life, the fear slowly dissipated. I began to more fully experience the joy of Michael. Even then, I knew that time would eventually run out, but I vowed that no matter how much time we had left, we would spend it in celebration.

This was not a one-time decision or one that came easily. It was a choice that I had to make over and over again, and in making that choice, little did I know that I was ultimately preparing myself for the most difficult choice of all: letting Michael go when the time came for his life to end at the age of twenty-seven.

How does one survive these types of stressors and the emotional highs and lows associated with them?

Each of us learns to manage, survive, and even thrive, in our own unique way. For us, Michael was a blessing. Yes, we encountered a multitude of negative emotions associated with time and money as we battled the many stressors associated with disability. Even so, we learned to make meaning from something that made no sense. We experienced the blessing and joy of Michael, and in doing so, to come to some deeper understanding of his purpose. For example, my newfound thought patterns eventually catapulted me into child and family advocacy work in Michael's early years whereas my husband was inspired to grow his business in an effort to meet our son's many needs.

The Impact of Society on Perspectives and Worldviews

Our perspectives and worldviews are influenced by several factors, from childhood storylines, to our surroundings, to the society around us. When you're working to develop greater self-awareness, it's important to consider the source of your beliefs. Contrast our meaning-making experience of Michael's life over the course of many years with a different conversation I had while visiting Sri Lanka. As a completely different culture from the United States, I anticipated that Sri Lanka would hold a different worldview about persons with disabilities. Thus, in a discussion with a leading Southeast Asian pastor there, I innocently asked what I thought was a simple question: "What is your philosophy here on disability?"

Because Sri Lanka is a shame-based culture, he explained, children with special needs are often viewed as punishment for something done in a past life. This is not to say that these parents don't love their children. But in a culture where financial resources are limited, it's not too difficult to imagine that these families face far greater challenges in rearing a child with a disability than someone in westernized society. Compound the financial issues with a cultural belief that your child is a burden and punishment for something you did in a prior life, and we can see a stark contrast between the perspective that your child is a blessing and the perspective that your child is a burden. A shame based culture might also posit a far greater challenge to becoming the director of your own movie.

While my worldview that Michael was a blessing clearly made my life easier and far more meaningful, we can't assume that the "burden" conversation is any less relevant or wrong. The point is—it's simply a different perspective based on a different worldview or experience of life. Our meaning-making systems are not necessarily right or wrong although they can be when we harm others. Rather, how we make sense of our world is often based on our developmental level of maturity, our ability to see the world through many different lenses, and from those lenses, to determine our own worldview—always open to yet new perspectives arising as we grow and mature to different levels.

All this being said, being the director of your own movie means paying closer attention to your thoughts and behaviors in relation to the daily circumstances of life. This capability will help you step into your biggest experience of life.

Utilize this Reflective Practice section to help you step into your biggest life via becoming the director of your own movie.

Reflective Practice:

Part III emphases the opportunity to step into your biggest life. Chapter 7 introduces the importance of learning to consciously observe yourself in the moment so that you can develop and grow and so that you can be more proactive in the choices you make.

The practice for this chapter focuses on *witnessing*. Witnessing has to do with our capacity to step outside ourselves in specific moments in order to observe our own thoughts or behaviors. Think of yourself as literally standing behind the camera watching yourself in action. As the director, you get to choose your response.

This is not a practice you will learn in one or two moments. It requires slowing down your thoughts and actions such that you can observe. It takes time and practice.

Begin with something routine or small. Over time, you'll be able to witness yourself in more stressful circumstances, and you'll ultimately find that you build a capability to more appropriately respond to the uncontrollable circumstances that may arise in your daily life.

Spend at least 21 days observing yourself in the moment. Each morning, select one activity that you will focus on for at least five minutes. For example, you might observe yourself having your morning coffee or shaving. Whatever activity you select, observe your thoughts, feelings, and actions. You might even try changing your normal course of action. What would the director have you do differently? Maybe you'll have your coffee in a quiet room instead of on the fly in the car. You get to choose the action and your response.

At the end of each day, spend 10-15 journaling your responses to the following questions:

- As you witnessed yourself during the chosen activity, what specific thoughts or emotions influenced your behaviors?
- What were the underlying assumptions or beliefs associated with those thoughts and behaviors?
- As the director of your own movie, what thoughts or assumptions would you have to let go of in order to be more proactive in the choices you make?

8

Pursue Time and Money in Healthier Ways

I f you've ever read a book or watched a movie about Mount Everest, you know that it's the highest mountain on earth.[24] At 29,029 feet above sea level, only select mountaineers dare trek the summit. In fact, over 250 individuals have died trying.[25] There's a reason for this. Climbing Mount Everest takes a significant amount of skill and determination.

So it is with human development. While most of us would like a better, different life, we simply don't know how to get there. Life can seem complex and hard. It's all we can do to get through our daily activities. Add to the equation the many stressors associated with time and money, and life can become darned right overwhelming. If you're focusing on getting your basic needs met, e.g., paying the mortgage and putting food on the table, there's often very little time for self-reflection, let alone the hoped-for experience of self-actualization.

Starting the ascent to a more meaningful, prosperous life involves slightly shifting gears from the *how* of self-awareness, which we have talked about already, to the *why*. I use the analogy of ascending a mountain because it's a very concrete way to wrap our minds around the essence of human development and *why* it's important for you to consider the climb you are about to embark on. As the director of your own movie, you can decide what mountain you want to climb and how far you want to go. The climb, however, is not something you can force. You can train yourself to reach that highest peak, but similar to the greatest mountain climber, there is never any guarantee that you'll get exactly where you want to go, exactly when you want to get there. Why? Because, as we all know, obstacles get in the way. Life gets in the way. How you undertake and make meaning from those obstacles will determine whether or not you realize the peak experience of your life.

The first step in being able to make meaning of those obstacles is to have a basic understanding of the *stages* of human development and how they impact your climb, in addition to the *lines* of human development, which we have already briefly discussed.

There was a time when leading theorists believed that we, as human beings, stopped developing around the age of twenty-one. What we now know, however, is that the process of human development continues across the lifespan. This is the good news for you and me because it means that these stages help us understand a scientific certainty: we can mature into new ways of thinking and being that will ultimately help us to change the direction of our lives.

Stages of Human Development

The field of human development, or what some leading theorists refer to as a constructive-developmental theory (CDT), explores how people develop and mature, how they construct or interpret their life experiences, and how those interpretations can change and become more complex over time.[26] The theory contends that a person's growth and development are processes whereby the individual adopts more complex ways of making meaning of life experiences.[27]

Sound familiar? This is pretty much what I've been alluding to throughout the course of this book. As we progress through the stages of human development, we experience our mind, body, and spirit on a deeper level. We begin to understand ourselves in the context of past, present, and future, and in doing so, we begin to make different choices. As the director of our own movie, we now have the power to change how we think, feel, and act in response to the world around us. As these developmental moves arise within us, we also have an opportunity to change our experience of time and money. Finally, as we progress through stages of maturity and human development, we become more complex and are consequently able to assess and address internal and external complexities to improve our lives for the better. We become better able to integrate and differentiate previous stages of development into a more complex understanding and experience of life.

As researcher Cynthia McCauley and her fellow colleagues state, "Constructive-developmental theory concerns itself with two primary aspects of development: (a) the organizing principles that regulate how people make sense of themselves and the world (orders of development) and (b) how these regulative principles are constructed and re-constructed over time (developmental movement)."[28]

So, what does this mean for you and me?

Our stage of development, as one dimension of who we are, determines how we experience life and how our mental processes or consciousness evolves. Additionally, it impacts how we engage in the process of self-awareness, our first step to meaningful change. In other words, as we progress through stages of human development, we experience life differently because we experience life from a different level of consciousness. No one stage of development is better than another, but understanding this evolutionary process may offer you important insights into how to make better choices in your life.

Let's get back to the mountain. Imagine yourself at the base of a majestic mountain. Now, imagine this mountain as having at least twelve separate base camps. Visualize each of these base camps as a stage of development. Again, one base camp isn't better than another. They're just different, and each offers up a different viewpoint of the valley below.

Some people will only climb to the first base camp and enjoy the view from there. Others will do additional hard work to continue on to the second, third, or perhaps even twelfth base camp.[29] While the climb upward and onward might feel more challenging, the main difference is the view. The first base camp is closest to the foot of the mountain, so those that decide to camp and stay there have somewhat of a limited perspective whereas those that travel onward and upward find that with each new elevation, they have a broader, perhaps even more fulfilling, viewpoint and perspective on the valley below.

When you develop greater self-awareness of your own thoughts and actions, you are positioned for the climb. You set yourself up to experience a later stage of development. Now, you can't expect to have the same experience of the summit, for example, if you arrive by helicopter. The rigors of the climb itself add to the experience. They are what help formulate your perspective for the next camp, thus making each camp, each stage, as important as the others. Finally, you can't get to the fourth base camp or beyond without first traveling through the first, second, and third any more than a baby can learn to run before he or she walks.

This, my friends, is an oversimplified example of what it means to move through the stages of human development. When we get into the habit of examining our own thoughts and behavior and learn to make meaning of those aspects of self in relation to our life circumstances, we have the potential to grow and develop to later stages. Even as the potential is there, we are vulnerable to the complexities of life. If, for example, I have some unresolved issues in my life that have not been addressed (as I did with respect to time and money and my parents' failure to provide either), those shadows will follow us throughout our journey. I still might be able to trek the mountain of life, but when I arrive at basecamp four, I will bring that shadow with me unless I've done the hard work of discovery and resolved that particular issue beforehand. When you're making this climb in consciousness, think of those "shadow" issues as rocks in your backpack. They will weigh you down and weaken your climb if they're left unaddressed.

Here again, however, is more good news. You don't need to do this hard work alone. Sometimes we get stuck at base camp because we don't know what else to do. Sometimes we get stuck because it's comfortable and safe, and we don't feel equipped to continue the journey. Or, sometimes the journey itself is frustrating and overwhelming. Whatever the reason, if you're stuck at the base of the mountain due to some level of trauma, pathology, or other life changing event, you can seek counseling or coaching to help you regain stability

All this to say, the path of human development is neither linear nor stagnant. We are works in progress. Even when our life circumstances or our unresolved shadows cause us to slide into an earlier stage, we know the path to the base camps above. We have experienced that altitude, witnessed that perspective, and we can use our knowledge and experience to help us regain our footing. Our earlier stage experiences give us the opportunity for a more complex understanding of life in our later stages. This is why we can often look back and learn something from our past. This is the good news. Every stage transcends (arises in complexity) and includes the previous stages. Here again, if we use our physical line of development as an example, we do not forget how to sit or stand when we learn to run or sprint.

The Big Connection between Stages of Human Development and the Chase.

As I've briefly alluded to before, understanding the basics of human development will tell you several important things that can help you end the unhealthy chase of time and money. First, research tells us that adults who are positioned at the earlier stages of development, for a variety of reasons, may have challenges related to how they think about and subsequently manage their time and money.[30]

Second, understanding the basics of human development will help you understand more about the people around you. Think about your teen-age daughter who recently spent her entire allowance on iTunes. You may have asked, "What were you thinking?" Or, maybe your son just can't seem to abide by your rule of being home by midnight. "I just lost track of time," he innocently tells you. You scratch your head in disbelief wondering, "How is this possible?"

It's possible because, literally speaking, adolescents rarely have a fully developed sense of time and money that are considered "responsible" by our more mature standards. They simply cannot see what we see. We understand these types of situations in terms of overall "maturity" but understanding them in terms of human development gives us more tolerance and compassion.

Let me add that stages of development, however, do not *necessarily* correlate with age. I have experienced many clients in their fifties that have a less-than-mature sense of time and money. Remember my example of David and how he viewed people with money as greedy and oppressive? This is why it's so important for us to examine our early-childhood stories with respect to time and money. In reflecting on those early experiences, we can sometimes unravel how we came to be where we are. We can then choose different patterns of thought and behavior; we can alter the course of our lives.

While I have offered up a hierarchal example of human development, in reality, there is an ebb and flow to how we develop, an unfolding, if you will, as our consciousness evolves into different worldviews and perspectives.[31] As preeminent philosopher and author Ken Wilber reminds us, within each stage, we embrace a different type of self-identity, a different type of self-need, and a different type of moral stance.[32] Thus, although thinking of human development as a trek up a mountain is a useful way to visualize this evolutionary process, having a more pronounced understanding of human development, to include the dimensions of lines, states, and types, will also provide value to anyone looking to achieve a better understanding of self in relation to their life experience.[33]

How States and Lines Affect Your Experience of Time and Money
States are something we experience under specific conditions. When you think of "states," imagine adding the phrase "of mind" or "of confusion" or "of fear." For example, you might experience a drug-induced state of mind or a state of fear or a state of impulsiveness. These are moments that often come and go, and while they have the potential to impact our overall development within any stage, we still have to grow, develop, and evolve in order for "altered states" to translate into a "permanent trait."[34]

In thinking about the three examples of states I've given above, we might imagine how a drug-induced state of mind or a state of fear, for example, could translate into an impulsive use of time and money. If on the other hand, you fall into impulsive spending or poor management of time on a consistent basis, this might suggest something beyond a temporary state. Consistent actions that are clouded by persistent fear or scarcity could be an indication of an early developmental perspective or even the presence of a pathological condition which may require some specific attention or professional intervention.

Human developmental *lines* relate to individual capabilities. I have discussed several lines of development in prior chapters to include the cognitive, interpersonal, spiritual, and moral. Wilber identified over twenty-four such capabilities,[35] six of which I utilize in my integral coaching and consulting practice: the cognitive, emotional, somatic, interpersonal, spiritual, and moral.[36]

Each of these capabilities arises independently within each person's stage of development.[37] An individual may, therefore, exhibit higher levels of cognitive development even as he or she simultaneously indicates lower levels of moral development. We might, for example, find ourselves facing a very smart, but spiritually and morally depraved, Hitler.[38] Also, all developmental lines travel independent of one another and cannot be compared to one another;[39] however, they all move in the same direction, that is, similar to stages of human development, developmental lines increase in complexity as you grow and mature.

Stages, states, and lines of development, and the distinctions between them, are important considerations that can help us grow up and mature into healthier perspectives on time and money. These distinctions help us understand more about the underlying complexity of ourselves and others. In doing so, we can make better decisions. For example, if I'm married to someone at a later stage of development, and my spouse has a broader cognitive understanding of the world than I do, we may interact well because my spouse is able to appreciate my point of view. He has already progressed through my stage.

However, because the lines of development arise independently from one another as well as within each stage, my spouse's cognitive stance may be at a higher level than his spiritual stance. He may have a broader cognitive ability, but, if my spiritual line of development has surpassed his spiritual development, he may not fully understand or agree with my spiritual viewpoint. In essence, the couple that is misaligned when it comes to stages and lines of development may find themselves in conflict in several areas.

Finally, how we come to make meaning and understand our world, means that we move in and out of healthy and robust perspectives on life. I might, for example, be at a later stage of development, but when life challenges hit, I can just as readily behave in compulsive or irrational ways with respect to my use of time and money. Given the many complex nuances between stages, states, and lines of development, is it any wonder that we can get into conflicting internal and interpersonal situations when it comes to time and money?

When you learn to be the director of your own movie, you can witness your own thoughts, feelings, emotions, perceptions, beliefs, and behaviors. You can watch your own experiences, as though watching through a camera lens, and you can adapt and adjust accordingly. You understand that these experiences are not something outside of you, but something inside of you. You're not an actor in a play. You are the director. You have the free will to choose different thoughts and thereby create different outcomes. You know that you're different than an alligator or a baboon. Life doesn't happen to you. You have the potential to make life happen.

Being the director of your own movie also means that you're willing to risk change. You're willing to risk looking through the camera lens directly into your experience of life such that you discover exactly where your mind, body, and spirit are fragmented. And, make no mistake about it, there is fragmentation that breeds deep within each of us. If we can agree, as I said earlier, that time and money are a window into the soul, then we can also agree that our brokenness can easily be exacerbated by misdirection of our time and money.

Being the director of your own movie also takes you beyond and outside a reactive state. Some will describe this experience as a hovering over, an eyewitness engagement of self over a conversation or situation rather than being actually in it. The director watches herself through the lens of life and cues herself via her own higher consciousness on how to respond. This represents a deep and profound sense of awareness such that one becomes greatly in-tune to the nuances of self in relation to the world around. Rather than react to the daily challenges of life, awareness allows us to be more fully present in the moment, to slow down the camera, if you will, take a deep breath, and exercise choice.

When we think about the profound impact of having the power of choice with respect to how we utilize two of our most important resources, time and money, the implications are significant. Understanding this significance is the difference between experiencing freedom and being stuck in a state of fear.

So, why engage in the climb of self-awareness? Why worry about stages, states, and lines? Because when we willfully engage and commit to the climb, when we become aware of where we are, where we want to go, and we learn how to get there, we transform our meaningful experience of life into emotional, spiritual, and even monetary riches. We experience greater prosperity in every sense of the word.

Reflective Practice:
Chapter 8 addresses the importance of pursuing healthier ways to experience time and money. This chapter's reflective practice focuses on *lines* of development as a way to engage in that ongoing healthy pursuit.

Review the descriptors of the six developmental lines described in Appendix D. Is there one specific line that might be holding you hostage with respect to time and money? For example, do you find it difficult to share your time with others (Interpersonal line)? Or, do you have a difficult time understanding why someone would contribute money to a homeless man on a street corner (Moral line)?

Determine one line of development that you would like to focus on for the next week. Make a list of all the ways this line supports you in

9

UNDERSTAND YOUR
DEVELOPMENTAL PERSPECTIVE

N ow that you have a broad understanding of human development, we're going to go a little deeper into the stages to help you identify where you might fall in the spectrum. Remember, one stage is not better than another, and the only way you can properly identify your specific stage is to take a valid and reliable assessment. The point of this segment is to help you begin to understand how the specific stages of development may impact one's experience of time and money. Researchers in the field have categorized the stages of human development into specific ways of thinking, or tiers, which I will describe in further detail below. In addition, the research points to clearly defined levels within each tier that indicate how people develop beginning with early-childhood through adulthood.

Before we take this deeper dive into human development, let me briefly share why I'm so passionate about your having this deeper understanding of your own developmental perspective.

In my many years as a professional speaker, consultant, trainer, and coach, I have had the unique privilege of working with thousands of people across North America. In this capacity, I have also enjoyed working with leaders in a variety of fields and industries to help them restructure their organizations and become more effective leaders.

One of the things that has struck me most in my extensive field experience is how hard people work. Yet, in the Leadership Development component of my business, I have also encountered countless people who are frustrated, angry, overwhelmed, overburdened, or on the verge of burnout. My Leadership Development sessions involve a rigorous process that is intentionally designed for personal and professional transformation. I love this aspect of my work because the process allows space for people to transform the way they think, live, and do business. Many years ago, however, I began to notice an interesting phenomenon: No matter how many people I worked with, no matter how rigorous the process, there was always one or two individuals who didn't seem able to make the shift. If there were hundred people in the room who rejoiced in all they had learned and the changes they had made, there would be one or two who just couldn't make the leap.

My curiosity was piqued.

When I began to explore human development in greater depth, I came to understand why. Our experience of life and our ability to receive new information such that we develop greater awareness and engage in transformational change is impacted by our current way of being, by our current stage of development. Change and growth requires that we visualize a new way of being, and this is a challenging endeavor. Most of us don't know how to engage in that level of work without a mentor, coach, or even a therapist to guide us. We just don't yet know how to right that ache in our belly. It's like slipping behind the driver seat of your first car, but no one's given you the keys.

As I've previously mentioned, there are specific dimensions of the stages that alert us to how we experience life. They also encompass our capacity to visualize the past, present, and future, our ability to prioritize and categorize ideas, assumptions, and judgments, and how we understand and value the perspectives of others. Each of these dimensions can have a direct impact on how we experience and utilize the resources of time and money. In order for you to gain some insight into your experience of time and money and the impact that experience may be having on your growth and development—on your ability to reach your highest potential—it is important for you to have, at the very least, some understanding of how these stages are represented.

Within each stage of human development, for instance, a person can have a specific time orientation and he may view the world from either an egocentric, ethnocentric, or world centric point of view. The twelve stages of development[40], as we currently understand them, encompass these world views and are often described within three specific tiers: The Concrete, the Subtle, and the Meta-Aware.[41] These tiers are important to our experience of time and money in that each tier represents how we engage in thought about the world we live in.[4] The complexities of all three tiers and the multiple stages within them are beyond the scope of this book. Suffice to say that the tiers and their respective stages offer valuable insight into how we make meaning in our individual worlds.

How the Stages Can Impact Your Experience of Time and Money

Current research points to twelve specific stages, four in each tier represented as the Concrete, the Subtle, and the Meta-Aware tiers. Approximately 94% of the US adult population[42] falls within five of

---

4   Appendix C offers a visual representation of how the stages are represented within each tier.

the stages, namely, The Conformist, Expert, Achiever, Pluralist, and Strategist stages. This percentage is also somewhat indicative of our westernized business culture, and as such, offers valuable insight into our own unique experience of time and money.

I will, therefore, offer a brief commentary on these five specific stages. Before I do, however, let me caution that it would not be useful for you to box yourself or anyone else into one of these categorical frameworks. While existing scoring protocols indicate that people fall into one of the stages, we never think, act, and behave from one stage all the time. Remember, the stages increase in complexity, and as we move into later stages of development, the dimensions of the earlier stages transcend and include the stages before. We may also have lines of development, e.g., our cognitive line, that cause us to map out into later stages of development. In my research on leaders, for example, I had some who measured at the Achiever stage of development[43], but many of their responses indicated thoughts and beliefs that mapped into the later stages of Construct-Aware. By the same token, I might score at one stage, and if some life circumstance hits me crossways, I can easily resort to thoughts and acts from an earlier stage.

Even so, within this fluctuation, we tend to operate primarily from one stage or another or from what most in the field refer to as our "Center of Gravity."

As I describe some of the dimensions of the stages in relation to time and money, also note that each stage is fully capable of having a meaningful and robust experience of time and money and life in general. I offer these subtleties only as a point of interest in the hopes that if you do catch a glimpse of yourself in either of these stages, particularly in relation to our earlier discussion on the scarcity perspectives, you will have some additional knowledge and guidelines for further exploration. My hope is that this information will encourage you to embrace transformational change so that you can make the dramatic shift toward more abundant perspectives.

The Conformist:

The Conformist stage is the last stage in the Concrete Tier. The three earlier stages represent babies and children and are not therefore relevant to this discussion. The Concrete Tier represents our ability to engage in *abstract thinking about concrete things.*[44] I can hold an apple in my hand and imagine how it will nourish my body. While the stages of development do not necessarily correlate to age, the earlier stages are often discussed in relation to years. For example, the people who measure at the Conformist stage most often fall within the teenage to thirty-something range. If you can recall your own teenage experiences or those of someone you know, you'll quickly remember that the focus at this age is more about approval from your peer group than it is about responsible behavior with respect to time and money. This is why your teenage daughter spends her entire allowance on iTunes or why your son never seems to make curfew.

Additionally, research indicates that the few adults, less than 12%[45] of the US population, who do fall within this range are not found in typical work environments. This is because they are often disabled by way of developmental delays or they simply have not yet fully matured. Those who never fully mature, often as a result of trauma or some environmental factor, e.g., violence or drugs, may even resort to some form of criminal activity. In other words, our prisons are full of people who have never been supported enough to cope with life in healthy ways or who have never learned to skillfully utilize their resources. For a variety of complex reasons, they simply haven't yet matured enough to make those types of responsible decisions. The example of David's story that I offered up in Chapter 5 is an example of a Conformist who, from a developmental perspective, never fully matured. As a result, David lived a life of high scarcity that resulted in financial chaos.

I mention the Conformist stage in the context of time and money because this segment of the population has a limited view of the past and the future. By this I mean, they more often than not see the past as being in front of them. The Conformist may live for today with immediate self-gratification as the norm. You will recognize these individuals because they tend to frequently speak about the past, and they do so with great energy often blaming those in the past for their own present circumstances. This is partially due to the fact that they live in the moment but are unable to plan for the future, so when the future becomes the present, they are often unprepared for whatever situation hits them. They also have difficulty prioritizing rules or the consequences of those rules. This propensity can essentially lead to a cycle of compulsive or addictive behaviors. The nature of these behaviors is an attempt to gain control over situations that seem out of control, and the scope and severity of those behaviors will vary depending on the peer group the person is associated with.

Additionally, the Conformist identifies with the rules of the community they are in, and if everyone around them behaves in irresponsible ways with respect to time and money, it is likely that they will follow suit. Because they need approval from the group, they may not have the wherewithal to make sound decisions on their own. Given this propensity, they may closely align with some of the high scarcity perspectives of time and money: lack of financial responsibility, to include consistent and ongoing debt/financial crisis, feelings of victimization with respect to financial circumstances, a tendency to make poor financial choices, bouts of egocentric spending, a survival mentality that inhibits the ability to visualize the future and make responsible choices. With respect to time, the Conformist may lack the ability to plan or focus. They may appear busy but are often less effective, and as such, they have a greater tendency to be crisis driven and unable to experience meaningful outcomes.

While we cannot stereotypically categorize all Conformists as people who live from a perspective of high scarcity, this is an egocentric stage, and the dimensions of self that are associated with this stage of development point to the potential for scarcity tendencies with respect to their experience of time and money. But, all is not lost. With the right interventions and support, an individual who measures as a Conformist and demonstrates these tendencies with respect to time and money can mature into healthier perspectives on time and money and life in general. The first step in doing so is to acknowledge any thoughts and behaviors associated with scarcity and seek appropriate guidance and counsel.

The Expert:

Thirty-six percent of the measured US population[46] falls within the Expert stage of human development. This stage is the first stage in the Subtle Tier which represents our potential to think in *concrete ways about abstract things*. This stage also represents a developmental movement to a third-person perspective that includes the beginning ability to self-reflect on one's own thoughts and feelings. However, juxtaposed against the Conformist, these individuals are capable of some level of introspection and self-understanding of their unique differences in relation to others, yet they are not ruled by the norms of the group. Additionally, this is an egocentric stage which means that while the Expert has some level of awareness of those around him, he may assume that others share his perspective or viewpoint. He may, therefore, try to change the collective to his point of view.

In terms of profession, Experts are often found in fields that require a high level of specific knowledge, e.g., engineering, law, health care, architecture, and finance. These people differentiate themselves from others by way of their expertise, and they tend to only rely on other experts for input. While people at this stage are adept at problem solving, they may not be able to fully view people/situations from multiple perspectives. They often believe that their solution is the "right" solution and may therefore demonstrate a tendency toward compulsive behavior and acts of perfectionism. Such acts can have a dramatic impact on their experience of time and money.

Our experience of time is related to our ability to recall the past, be present to the moment, and to visualize the future. For the Expert, perfectionism is counter-productive to their experience of time in that they have a tendency to place efficiency before effectiveness. What this essentially means is that they can easily get lost in the details of their work, miss the big picture, micromanage, and may even have difficulty prioritizing or meeting deadlines. The basic time orientation of the Expert allows him to see both the past and the present within a two-to-three-year timeframe, however, perfectionism can often catapult the Expert into analysis paralysis that results in little to no time/money capacity.

For the Expert, moderate scarcity perspectives are somewhat balanced in that they do exhibit Sporadic Generosity with respect to time. The Expert will give of his time and he will consistently be *on* time as a way to honor his commitments, but his inability to prioritize may also make it challenging for him to make time for family. The Expert's constant need for perfectionism and greater efficiency point toward the potential for moderate scarcity perspectives of time and money.

From this worldview, money requires effort, so work and financial responsibilities are burdensome. He therefore may not enjoy money because he is fearful of not having enough resources to meet his own needs. Moderate scarcity, with respect to money, however, shows up in his ability to exhibit a level of Forced Generosity. While the motives underlying the Expert's generosity may stem from a need to do the right thing or give to others because he wants some form of recognition, he is at least able to step outside his own comfort zone and any fear of not having enough to offer up his resources to others. The additional good news is that because the Expert relies on the expertise of others, he may have a greater tendency to seek outside counsel with respect to his finances.

The Achiever:

The Achiever stage, as the second stage in the Subtle Tier, represents approximately 30% of the US adult population.[47] This is also an egocentric stage, but in this case, the Achiever's third person perspective shows up as competitiveness. The Achiever can visualize five years into the future. Even so, she is consistently focused on goals and objectives so there is a propensity to chase time and money.

With this level of goal orientation and such a strong desire for success, the Achiever is great at strategically planning their use of time and money; however, because they are so driven, they may also struggle with balancing work and family. Whereas the Expert gets sidetracked by perfectionism, the Achiever gets sidetracked by taking on too many projects and deadlines. At this egocentric stage, it is also easy to lose track of time and money outside the scope of business since the primary focus is often on business results.

In terms of profession, this stage is often represented by leaders in politics or corporate environments, high level entrepreneurs, high fashion, the entertainment industry, or the more recent mega-successes of those in content marketing or high-tech companies. Juxtaposed against the Expert, the Achiever focuses on effectiveness over efficiency. They get things done and make things happen. Their hyper-individualism, however, can lead to isolation and separation.

Given these specific characteristics of the Achiever, it is not hard to imagine them fluctuating somewhere between the Moderate Scarcity to Moderate Abundance perspectives on time and money. This fluctuation would depend on how well business goals and objectives are being realized.

If business is booming, for example, the Achiever might align more closely with the Moderate Time Scarcity mantra, "*Time is fleeting. I should manage it well*," whereas the money soundbite might include the language, "*I have the ability to create the money I need for a better future.*"

More specific to time, the Achiever's ability to focus can lead to a sense of control over their own time, but when the pace gets too fast, they may fail to achieve their goal of life balance and readily fall into thoughts of scarcity or even burnout. In this regard, the Achiever may enjoy Intentional Generosity with respect to time, but their desire for meaningful time with family and loved ones may be jeopardized by their work commitments and their desire to achieve more success.

With respect to money, when the Achiever lives from the Moderate Money Abundance perspective, they view money from a neutral perspective. In other words, they do well to understand the flow of money, and they view money as an exchange for goods and services. They are often successful because they readily assume financial responsibility and save, spend, and invest wisely. However, their competitive spirit may result in workaholic behaviors and use of money as a source of power. Additionally, the Achiever may have a tendency toward Selective Generosity which means that they will contribute their financial resources if they have an abundance of money or as long as such giving does not interfere with their own goals, objectives, or lifestyle.

A Brief Caveat:

Before I move into the last two relevant stages of development, let me offer a brief reminder: The stages are not hierarchal in nature, and they do not necessarily correlate to my research on time and money in the traditional sense. I offer the relationship between the stages and the spectrum of time and money so that you can more clearly understand how developmental stages and the time/money storylines may be potentially related.[5] It is for you to determine where you fall on the spectrum in relation to both of these components.

Remember, as we move up our imaginary mountain of stages, there is an ebb and flow to our reality. If I am a woman who measures at a later stage of development, for example, I might enjoy all that this stage encompasses. I might also live from a high abundance time/money storyline. If, however, I suddenly become a widow only to wake up one morning and realize that I have been stripped of my financial stability, I might find myself operating from scarcity. I might even resort to what I knew in my earlier stages. If I do this in positive ways, all is good. But, if I resort to unhealthy perspectives, or what some therapists call a shadow crash, I may resort to fear and scarcity until I can "remember" myself in my full capacity at the later stage.

I suggest that you avoid any tendency to box yourself into one specific category. We are complex beings. Each stage and line of development has its strengths and weaknesses. My goal is to spark awareness so that you can embrace opportunity for change.

---

5   If you're interested in knowing your specific stage of development, you may access the assessment I mentioned earlier at *www.PacificIntegral.com*.

With this caveat in mind, let's move on to the last two stages.

The Pluralist:

The Pluralist represents the seventh stage of human development. It is in the Subtle Tier with an estimated US population of 11%.[48] It is also the first stage in the Subtle Tier that emphasizes the collective. If we return to our imaginary climb up the mountain of human development, you can see that the population of individuals who actually make the trek is limited. This is because few people understand how to engage in the transformational practices required to get there. You can also imagine that people at this stage of development have the potential for a broader perspective with respect to life and even time and money.

This is, in part, because people who measure at this stage have the potential to visualize the past and present within a ten-year time frame. This capacity alone points to the potential to embrace more abundant perspectives because while these individuals can learn from the past and prepare for the future, they also have the potential to be present in the moment. This potential diminishes the chase for time and money and positions the Pluralist for less anxiety and frustration in the midst of day-to-day life.

This stage also represents a 4th person perspective and an ethnocentric viewpoint which means that the Pluralist has a greater concern for harmony and equality within the community-at-large. Given this perspective, the Pluralist may be more inclined to live from a High Money Abundance. Juxtaposed against the Achiever, the identity of the Pluralist is not linked to how much money they actually have. They know they are able to construct their own reality and this may also include the ability to create the money they need and the desire to share it with others for the greater good.

Within this 4th person perspective, the Pluralist also recognizes that the interpretations of people and situations depend on the position of the observer. Whereas the Conformist may look to her past as a source of blame for present circumstances, the Pluralist believes she can construct her own reality and influence what she observes. The Pluralist also has a desire to test her own assumptions and to free others from limiting judgments or negative behaviors that work against the greater good, e.g., acts of greed.

I once had a client, for example, who was a very high level attorney. Due to her role within her law firm, she had no doubt once lived from an Expert and Achiever stage. When I met her, however, she was no longer concerned with participating in partner meetings or in any efforts that positioned her "to look good" amongst her peer group. As a Pluralist, she expressed an authentic sense of self that was now more dedicated to fighting on behalf of her clients' rights to include that which was right and just for the great good of the community. In this context, her relationship with the client was more important than the goal of making more money or her own critical acclaim.

In terms of professions, we often find the Pluralists in consulting, the helping professions, or human rights' endeavors. Bill Gates might also serve as an example of an Achiever who matured to a Pluralist in that he utilizes his financial wealth to now impact world hunger and education in developing countries via The Bill and Melinda Gates' Foundation.

Because the Pluralist values the relationship or the process over the goal, she may also experience greater freedom to choose how she utilizes time. Even at the Pluralist stage, however, this approach can be problematic in that the Pluralist values the multiple perspectives of others. While this can be a great way to gain valuable insight, there is a downside of this present-in-the-moment approach in that a Pluralist leader can easily alienate the Experts and Achievers on the team. In supporting what the others deem as unnecessary dialogue in meetings that go on ad infinitum, the Pluralist risks losing credibility among her peer group. For the Expert or Achiever in the room, such behavior is often viewed as poor leadership, an inability to move the group forward, and even indecisiveness. For the Pluralist who enjoys being fully present in the moment, it is important to notice that such an approach to time can prove to be extremely frustrating for those in their midst.

Even so, the Pluralist's desire to be fully present also contributes to a propensity toward High Time Abundance perspectives such that she experiences gratitude and joy for every moment. The Pluralist may also rarely feel guilt or shame when they take time for rest and recreation with others. Additionally, they have the capacity to see parent/child relationship across the lifespan. This supports the capacity for a generous spirit in relation to time as set forth in Appendix B in that they will be more apt to give freely of their time to family and those in need without expressed feelings of guilt or shame. This deep and abiding sense of family and community as a priority may contribute to Pluralist's express desire for inner peace, contentment, and joy.

The Strategist:

The Strategist stage is not to be confused with someone who is a strategic thinker as strategic thinking can occur in the earlier stages. For example, someone at the Achiever stage may strategically discern what must be accomplished whereas the Strategist is more concerned with a way of being in the world. This *being* is more about how to live in awareness such that his values and principles benefit the greater good of humanity.

This stage is represented by approximately 5% of the US adult population and is also the last stage in the Subtle Tier. As such, it represents a 4th person perspective from a collective stance. For the Strategist, however, the collective is not necessarily a person so much as it is a complex planet-centric network of systems. Additionally, the Strategist has access to a multi-generational, 25-year time span. Because he can see the complexity of multiple systems and because he can experience time in terms of past and future generations, the Strategist has the capacity to explore the dynamics of meaning-making in the context of the larger system and to effect or influence the container of those systems. This perspective, under healthy conditions, might therefore support the Strategist in a more robust experience of time and money because he might also see the importance of stewardship from an economic, ecological, and environmental perspective. In other words, the Strategist might be more inclined to consider his use of time, money, and other resources in terms of the impact on future generations. Even as the Strategist can learn from the past and see into the future, they are also quite able to experience time in the moment. Given this propensity, the Strategist is good at prioritizing competing commitments, opinions, and even beliefs because he recognizes the potential for growth and change in all things.

All of these factors, to include the willingness to support the growth and development of others, may also indicate a proactive, creative, and more holistic stance with respect to time and money as expressed in the High Abundance storylines. Accordingly, the Strategist might also have a greater propensity to contribute money from a Generous Heart to those in need and to freely offer up time to family and friends absent the expressed negative feelings of guilt, shame, or frustration that people in the earlier stages often experience.

The Meta-Aware Tier:

The final Meta-Aware Tier represents the capacity to think in *abstract ways about abstract things*. The final four stages in the Meta-Aware Tier, namely, the Construct-Aware, Transpersonal, Universal, and Illumined, represent less than 1% of the US population.[49] Because there are so few measured within these stages, however, we know very little about their perspectives. Suffice to say that people who measure in these later stages are able to witness their own projections in the moment, and they have a broader awareness of their thoughts and actions such that they may be more readily able to let go of negative storylines related to their time/money experiences.

The point is to honor what stage of development you're in because within each stage, we have the capacity to create a more robust experience of life by way of witnessing and understanding who we are, by addressing our shadow issues, and by embracing more abundant storylines with respect to our use of time and money.

Reflective Practice:

The focus of this chapter was to dive a bit deeper into the *stages of human development.*

For purposes of this reflective practice, I encourage you to review the stages as I've discussed them in this chapter. Chances are you can see yourself across multiple stages. Highlight specific elements of these stages in terms of your experience of time and money. Do these elements map across multiple stages or are you seeing yourself primarily land in one?

Select one element in your predominant stage to focus on. For example, if you see yourself in the Expert category, you might want to focus on how you prioritize your tasks each day. If you see yourself in the Achiever stage, you might want to examine how your goal orientation is impacting your ability to balance work and family.

Once you've selected one stage and the element you want to focus on, spend at least one week witnessing your own thoughts and behaviors with respect to this element.

Then, spend at least 15 minutes each evening journaling responses to the following questions:

- What element of which stage did you focus on?
- What did you notice about yourself in relation to your experience of time and money?

- What patterns associated with that experience are indicators of scarcity thinking?
- What patterns associated with that experience moved you closer toward abundance?

10

TREK THE PATH TO FREEDOM

There is an order to our world. Planets don't fall out of the sky and land on our rooftops. Dogs don't suddenly turn into cats. The universe, in all its complexity, self-organizes chaos, and from that chaos emerges order once again.[50]

So, it should be with your life. When you understand who you are in relation to your current circumstances, and chaos emerges—and it will emerge because that is the nature of order and chaos—you can willfully return your life to some form of purposeful rhythm. I think of this outcome as "having your house in order" which essentially means that you play by the rules of abundance. You play a responsible game of time and money such that you experience freedom over fear. You're not plagued by the chase. Time and money don't control you. You have mastery over time and money.

Understanding who you are within your current circumstances doesn't mean you're living the perfect life or that your bank account is overflowing with cash or that you can spend endless months basking in the sun on a remote Caribbean island. I'm not talking about utopia. I'm talking about wisdom, discernment, and taking responsibility for the choices you make. I'm talking about a sense of order that arises out of your heightened awareness of the dimensions of self and your commitment to a robust and healthier way of life.

We all have trials and tribulations that hit our lives from time to time. No one is immune to the challenges of life. Remember, the difference is not what comes our way. The difference lies in how we think about our circumstances. What matters is how we respond and how we make sense of those unique, sometimes challenging, opportunities for growth. Additionally, having your house in order means that you're ready to move through life with a sense of freedom and abundance such that you realize greater prosperity in your life.

How, then, can you intentionally effectuate such a possibility?

Implementing Your Path to Freedom

Up until this point, we've primarily been focusing on awareness. What are you thinking about time and money, and how is this thinking translating into your actions or behaviors?

Now that you have examined how your thought patterns with respect to time and money translate to behaviors, we can shift gears and return once again to our earlier conversation on the basic premise that "where your treasure lies, there you heart will be also."[51]

The challenge here is to pay close attention to your utilization of time and money because your choices and actions speak directly to what really matters to your heart. When your heart and mind are in alignment, your spirit will soar. Therein lies the freedom.

Freedom from the chase in no way implies that we end our pursuit of time and money. That would prove impossible. What it means is that we embody a healthier approach to time and money such that we experience a more robust life. There are many paths to this experience. Our exploration into human development is one integrated path that supports our growth into freedom and abundance. But this path requires that we not only change our thinking, we must also "do" something along the way if we want to experience different results. In the field of human development, we speak about such *doing* as "practices." A golfer, for example, doesn't just *think* about playing golf. In order to be a better golfer, he must *practice* it. So it is with human development. We have the unique opportunity to engage in specific practices that further enhance our stages, states, and lines of human development.

With respect to your utilization of time and money, one significant practice that can help you further develop the dimensions of self as we have discussed them is the practice of *stewardship*.

Embrace a disciplined practice of stewardship as it relates to time and money, and I can promise you a dramatic shift in your life. Why? Because all acts of stewardship produce a cycle of generosity, gratitude, compassion, and ultimately greater love for self, others, and, depending on your chosen spiritual path, even God and greater humanity.

Stewardship, I have discovered, is the secret to a more meaningful, prosperous life. Before I give you some ways to engage in such a practice, let's first examine the essence of stewardship from both a secular/scientific and spiritual perspective.

Stewardship: A Spiritual Term for the Secular World

In his revised edition of *Stewardship*, author Peter Block speaks to the need for greater stewardship in relation to the distribution of power, purpose, and reward within our institutional settings.[52] He defines stewardship as the *holding on to something in trust for another*, further stating, "There are growing questions in society about the relationship between our institutions and the environment, the disparity in wealth, our health, and other social concerns . . . ."[53] Block goes on to say that while all of these were once questions of marginal consideration, they are now vital to our collective survival and well-being. Stewardship, he adds "is a narrative of abundance: it says that what we have is enough, that there are limits to growth, and it expands our field of vision to care for something larger than profitability."[54]

While Block speaks more specifically to issues associated with corporate governance and sustainability, stewardship is equally important to us as individuals because stewardship suggests that the "answer to our economic problems is not reduced to costs or [more money]; it is to focus on relationships, reciprocity"[55] and our own participation and accountability. After all, it is *our* collective survival and well-being that is at stake, is it not? Are we not the ones who contribute to the collective society? Our contribution, then, is directly influenced by our capacity for stewardship. Furthermore, stewardship is a premise, a way of life that has a history, one that far outdates our modern-day corporate complexities.

Briefly going beyond Block's secular discussion of stewardship to the foundational definitions that are grounded in various spiritual and religious traditions offers additional value for the practice of stewardship. In spiritual traditions, stewardship initially had more to do with the utilization of resources, such as time, money, and talent, in ways that honored God and served a greater good. Today, however, the construct has evolved and is considerably broader in that it is strongly associated with issues of sustainability and the importance of linking spirituality and stewardship to financial decision-making.[56]

Perhaps this linkage between sustainability, spirituality, and stewardship is being re-birthed at just the right time. Again, we can look to the turmoil on Wall Street in 2008 and the teetering collapse of multiple global economies as examples of the negative consequences that flow from an absence of stewardship. The instability of these economies was spearheaded, for the most part, by irresponsible acts of corporate and banking greed. These acts and the resultant outcomes represent scarcity and fear at the most extreme levels.

Yet, all is not lost. Remember, even chaotic environments have the potential to self-organize. These examples stirred up research and ongoing interest about the need for spirituality in corporate environments. How much more important is it, then, for us, as leaders, business owners, and responsible citizens to embrace the idea of developing our spiritual and moral lines, and, along with it, incorporate the practice of stewardship into our lives? Allow me to suggest that we can no longer ignore the practice of stewardship or our own spiritual development in our businesses since it "provides the ultimate foundation for moral behavior."[57] The ongoing and persistent threats to our society suggest that the time to embrace the concept of stewardship is now.

Stewardship, as it's now linked to sustainability, also suggests that we preserve the world's natural resources for the next generation. It's the reason we care about emissions, recycling, and the materials we use to bring our hamburgers home from the drive through. In this context, we "make decisions and take actions that are in the best interests of future generations as well as current generations."[58] Stewardship and spirituality both embody a very direct and concrete balance between our egocentric selfish desires and a desire to serve the greater good.

Here's what researchers McCuddy and Pirie have to say about the connectedness of spirituality and stewardship:

> Being spiritual requires human beings to approach the consumption of goods and the accumulation of wealth in a different manner. These economic activities should not take place to maximize one's utility to the exclusion of others'

interests. Rather, they should occur in the context of sharing and helping others improve their situation in life. With the guidance of spirituality, the consumption of goods, the accumulation of wealth, and the sharing of wealth should be done for the common good.[59]

By contrast, the absence of stewardship can lead to extreme scarcity and our need to control things that are out of our control. That need for control often evolves from a failure to exercise stewardship simply because it doesn't fit into our basic logical box of understanding. In this context, the basic economic principal of years past implies that "the only way I can win is if you lose." Some people couch this mentality as promoting healthy competition, but, recent events tell us that such a perspective is not always so healthy. By contrast, the practice of stewardship contends that the world is better off when each of us balances resources for the greater good. Sometimes, the benefit of that greater good is within your own family, your own life. Sometimes, it's about doing what's best for the nation or our society as a whole.

An important note about stewardship, however, is that it's not to be confused with the economic principal of socialism. Stewardship does not ask a central decision maker to determine who gets what. Stewardship results in actions based on a diverse population's genuine attempts to share information, resources, time, money, and talent with the intention of producing more of the same.

We see the results of this type of collaborative effort quite eloquently displayed in today's marketplace as content marketers have set a new trend in business. "Content is king," they exclaim.[60] This mantra represents a commitment to the sharing of information, at no cost, and yes, this sharing is intended to eventually capture a following for future sales. It's capitalism at its best. The difference is, these Internet marketers are collaborating with one another to increase their customer bases.

Another example is a community-based restaurant row where business leaders are not so much in competition with one another as they are leveraging their resources of time and money to draw more people to one specific area. The underlying theme of stewardship, in these scenarios, fully meets our definition of developing abundance by working towards a greater good for a population that is bigger than the individual actors. Simply put, there are enough resources to go around, and each of us, in our own unique way, can contribute to the greater whole. When I win, you win. *We* win, everybody wins.

We can be good stewards of our time and money just as we can be good stewards of our natural resources, e.g., earth, water, air. In fact, the spiritual and secular discussions of stewardship both call upon us to do so. Most of us can quite readily buy into the secular perspective of stewardship because we have evolved to a people who realize the need to preserve these natural resources, stop pollution, and reduce and reverse global warming. But, if time and money are running us ragged, if they are the source of our stress and physical and emotional imbalances, isn't it wise to have the same level of concern about these most important resources as well? What this essentially means is that we are challenged to examine our heart and determine what's most important to us.

The concept of stewardship can be applied to all aspects of life: the environment, economics, health, property, information, and even theology. From a theological perspective, for example, stewardship asks us to become a person of character who loves God and others more fully. Words like "responsibility" and "obedience" are part of the quest for stewards.

The premise of stewardship is so important, in fact, that many of the ancient traditions have something to say about it in one form or another. Biblical scripture, for example, speaks to the proper use of money, the stewardship of money, no less than 2,350 times.[61] The ancient Hindu

Vedas address the flow of money—the wisdom in knowing when to hold it and when to let go.

In my own spiritual tradition, stewardship, means that everything—the earth, all our money and possessions, cars, bank accounts, investment properties—everything technically belongs to God because he is the creator of all things. He desires that we live a life of abundance, but basically, all that we have and own technically belongs to the creator. We have dominion over the earth, but we also have a responsibility to take care of that which is entrusted to us.

If you're like most people, this is a tough pill to swallow. Our internal dialogue screams, "Wait a minute! I work hard for what I have. I've earned every penny, every single asset, every single personal belonging. And, my time is my own to do with as I please. I work hard every day, and I deserve to do what I want to do with my time and my money."

This is a perfectly natural response. We are, after all, people who like our stuff, as American comedian George Carlin used to say. But, think about the shift required to embrace this level of stewardship, of acting for the benefit of the greater good. Think about the level of freedom associated with knowing that you don't have to hold on to every possession–that you can be generous with your time and even your money. When we actively engage in acts of stewardship that allow us to do more for others, we actually reap multiple benefits.

The opportunity that we have to hold our resources in trust for someone else[62] requires a significant shift in thinking. It requires us to recognize that "stuff" doesn't have to own us or our emotions. When we hold the perspective that we are "entrusted" to care for our resources, we quite simply make different choices. The steward bears the responsibility of *caring for* time and money without the burden of being *controlled by* time or money. The steward is thereby empowered to be the director of her own movie not just in terms of how she witnesses her own thoughts and behaviors, but also in terms of how she behaves in relation to her use of time and money.

The following discussion on the ethical nature of stewardship might also help you appreciate the importance of adopting a practice of stewardship in your personal and professional life so that you can step into a life of radical abundance.

Stewardship: An Ethical Perspective

Another way to think about stewardship is as an ethical way of handling your resources, a mindset, if you will, that embodies the responsible planning and management of resources under our control. Such resources include time, talent, and possessions such as money and property. Stewardship, in this context, is "a protective restraint, a taking care of resources through nurturing and thrifty management of their use."[63]

When we take on responsibility for what we receive, how we utilize those resources, and how we ultimately share them with others, we begin to embrace a stewardship mindset that supports us in more abundant thought. Authors McKnight and Block refer to this process as the difference between consumerism versus citizenship.[64]

Stewardship allows people to overcome the fear of the scarcity

No matter how close we are to living from a perspective of abundance, it only takes one negative moment to snap us back into scarcity thinking. There is hope, however, because we can change our perspectives. We can break the cycle of scarcity.

The practice of good stewardship is one direct way to do just that. When we engage in acts of stewardship, we naturally adopt more abundant perspectives that erase our fear of not having enough. By "acts" of stewardship, I mean that we are willing to reexamine our beliefs about time and money and how we utilize those resources.

Additionally, stewardship is vitally important because when we engage in a perspective of abundance, we create abundant communities.[65] In doing so, we benefit ourselves, and we help to create a sustainable future for generations to come.[66]

Bottom line: Stewardship and the outcome of abundance are important to your children, your grandchildren, their children, and on it goes. The alternative is we just gobble up one another with greed as a side dish.

Think about the possibility of a world where everyone operates from a perspective of stewardship and the freedom of abundance. We would live beyond the negative mantra of "*The only way I win is if you lose.*" Rather, we would all come from a sense of abundance such that we wisely use the resources we have, and together, we would creatively solve our most challenging problems.

Reflective Practice:
Chapter 10 addresses the practice of stewardship as the secret to a more meaningful and prosperous life. This practice is designed to help you examine your own *potential for stewardship*. Take some time by yourself to journal responses to the following questions in an effort to help you gain greater insight into your existing paradigms with respect to stewardship:

- What is your criteria for contributing financial resources to others?
- In what specific ways do you intentionally earn, spend, and save money?
- In what ways do you respond to people outside your inner circle who may require your time?
- How do you demonstrate generosity of time and money to the people you love—your spouse, children, family, and friends?

- In what specific ways do you utilize your resources of time and money for the greater good?
- On a scale of 1 to 10, where do you rate from negative to positive with respect to your understanding of stewardship and how you're living it out in your daily life?

Part IV

THE SOLUTION: SHIFTING TO A PARADIGM OF RADICAL ABUNDANCE

11

A New Perspective on Money

B arry was the kind of client that every consultant dreams about having. He was soft-spoken yet direct in his communication. As president of an established architectural and engineering firm, he was clear on his values. He cared deeply about his two partners and his employees, and he knew where he wanted to take the company. More importantly, he lived from a perspective of abundance. I first noticed how this perspective played out when I learned that he had instituted a company policy for the office to close at noon on Fridays. Barry believed that the employees needed extra time for things like golf or maybe just tossing a baseball around with one of their children.

Barry also demonstrated specific acts of stewardship at a personal and professional level. His employees were well-paid, his clients well-serviced, his prices modestly competitive. He generously supported many nonprofit efforts in the local community, and he always had time for questions or concerns from his team members no matter how many deadlines he was facing or how much stress he was experiencing.

I was blessed to work with Barry and his team over the course of several years. Because Barry also believed in investing in his employees, I was brought in to engage the team in leadership development. Barry, you understand, was committed not only to the growth and development of his company; he was also committed to the growth and development of his people. Rarely in my career have I had the opportunity to witness a leader with a more abundant perspective on time and money.

In reliving my experience with this most extraordinary leader, it wouldn't be a leap to state that Barry epitomized Peter Block's corporate stewardship model as referenced in chapter 10. He consistently questioned how he might better distribute power, purpose, and reward within the company's infrastructure. And, there was another measure of his abundant spirit. Sometimes the measure of a man is attributed to the company he keeps. Barry was blessed in that he had two other highly responsible partners who also shared his perspectives on stewardship. Together, these three men demonstrated the cycle of generosity, gratitude, compassion, and love that comes as a result of good stewardship.

You see—all three partners believed that the company's success was a blessing. They worked hard, shared the wealth, valued and respected their employees, loved their wives and children, were God-fearing men, and as a result of their goodness, they created meaningful employment and prosperity for a great many people— including me. With this blessing, however, came a great responsibility that was never taken lightly. These partners carried the weight of *holding on to something in trust for another*—those others being their employees, each other, their clients, their families, their community, and ultimately, their God.

Some people assume it's easy to come from abundance when your business is doing well. This is true. However, I witnessed one of the most dramatic examples of a stewardship worldview amongst these three partners during the market crash of 2008.

Unfortunately, the firm was greatly impacted by the train wreck in the housing market. It would have been easy for Barry and his partners to shift into hatchet-firing practices as so many other firms were doing. After all, with over fifty employees, a large office, and their own three families at stake, they could have cut their losses early and simply let everyone else go.

By contrast, another one of my corporate clients, who had yet to develop a practice of stewardship and was still stuck in a scarcity mindset, took the opposite approach. Their leadership chose to send out memos instructing specific people to bring their laptops and their office keys to room 222 on sequential Thursday afternoons. After the second week of cutbacks, people quickly figured out the game plan. Fear and scarcity ran rampant throughout the company as twenty-plus-year employees, many of them couples, witnessed their friends, colleagues, and eventually themselves, be thoughtlessly discarded like yesterday's trash.

Eventually, however, the reality of the market was too much for Barry and his two partners. The greater good, they realized, required them to cut back, and they approached me with heavy hearts. As Barry began to consider what must be done, my mind flashed to his office Christmas party just a few years prior. We both sat and marveled at all the young men with their wives. I remember saying something to the effect, "All these young families that you're impacting—look what you guys have built." He nodded in agreement, but even then, I could sense the burden he was carrying. The economy was already beginning to shift, and while none of us yet knew the impact of these changes, it was clear that Barry carried the weight of what was yet to come.

And, now here we were, a few short years later . . . talking about downsizing.

"These guys are like family to us," Barry shared. "We need to come up with a strategy on how to downsize with as little pain as possible."

As it turned out, the process was long and indeed painful as the market continued to rear its ugly head. The amount of cutbacks was minimized as much as possible, and as each person was terminated, they were sent off with grace, dignity, and a promise that should things turn around, and they so desired, they were welcomed to return. I was in the office on one such day, and I can honestly say that I've never witnessed anything quite like it. The collaboration and camaraderie were unsurpassed. Barry and his partners had built up so much good will through years of stewardship and abundant thinking that they avoided the same toxic environment that my other client experienced. Their colleagues gave them the benefit of the doubt that they had tried everything they could short of layoffs. Watching the emotions, respect, and even the love jointly expressed was something I'll never forget.

The market turned around a bit too late for Barry's firm, and I'm sure some employees may have resented that they were terminated. The next several years were not easy for Barry and his partners, but they weathered the storm and never abandoned their commitment to stewardship nor did they lose sight of their abundant perspectives. Enough was enough until the business was sold to a national firm. Then, they picked themselves up, dusted off, and began to create all over again.

It's doubtful I'll ever experience a team quite like these three partners again. I learned a lot from them, in particularly, that abundance combined with stewardship produces resiliency, creativity, meaningful relationships, and a robust way of tackling life even when—no, especially when—the world flips upside down.

This dichotomy between scarcity and abundance is profound. The question is not whether or not we'll face adversity; we most certainly will. The question is more about how we will rise up: Will we allow the beast of scarcity and fear to consume us, or will we embrace abundant acts of stewardship and allow them to carry us through?

We've discussed the High-to-Moderate Scarcity storylines that have surfaced as result of my research and field experience. Let's now explore the Moderate-to-High Abundance end of the spectrum. Contrary to the negative emotions that arise when we live in scarcity, the abundance storylines indicate feelings of satisfaction, happiness, balance, and fulfillment, even expressions of peace, contentment, and joy. Such positive emotions point to a far greater potential to step into a more abundant experience of money.

Moderate Money Abundance Storyline #1:
I have the ability to earn the money I need for a better future.

Before we move into the first money abundance storyline, allow me to once again call your attention to the fact that we are now shifting from a moderate scarcity perspective to a moderate abundant worldview. The reason for this is because the findings of my work to date suggest that there is a continuum of experience. I speak to this continuum in terms of "moderate" scarcity and abundance because the research suggests that one does not jump from high scarcity perspectives on time and money to high perspectives of abundance. Growth and development take time and a commitment to change in order to transform our thoughts from scarcity to abundance. There are, therefore, very subtle nuances that exist between the two moderate perspectives, some of which I will outline in this chapter. It's also important to remember that we may shift back and forth between scarcity and abundance depending on our life circumstances and the "states" in which we might find ourselves as we move through transitions in life. Here again, the point is not to box ourselves into one particular perspective so much as it is to develop awareness about when we fall into patterns that no longer support our practice of stewardship or our opportunities for greater prosperity.

This first money abundance storyline, therefore, is evidence of a *moderate* sense of abundance. People who embrace this first storyline view money as a tool to achieve a better end. They may not demonstrate as much emotion about money as someone who indicates a scarcity perspective. Their childhood stories are most likely centered on the importance of a great work ethic. However, unlike the moderate mindset of scarcity, this perspective on hard work is not fear-based. Rather, it comes from a stance of capability. What this essentially means is that people who live from this theme strongly believe in their own capacities to earn the financial resources they need, and in doing so, to have better futures.

In the moderate range, they may also have a slight tendency toward scarcity, and this tendency may be linked to a belief that people with money have more power. When they are at the peak of their earning, they may have a tendency to overspend so as to appear more like those in power. After a cycle of such overspending, they may experience guilt or shame at having been so frivolous. Additionally, their identity may be closely linked to how much money they actually have.

There are many good things about scoring within the range of Moderate Abundance with respect to money. However, even within this range, the subtle nuances of scarcity can surface. The dangers of these nuances are, in many ways, even more destructive than those associated with scarcity. The reason for this is because it's easy to convince ourselves that the thoughts and actions associated with this perspective are noble.

Within this first storyline of Moderate Money Abundance, let's examine two key perspectives that are showing up in my research. Please consider how these perspectives may be affecting your own personal or professional life and how they may contribute to your negative and positive outcomes with respect to money.

Perspective No. 1: The Industrious Worker Bee

Someone with this perspective is like a worker bee who believes *if it's to be, it's up to me*. When we live out of a conversation that we can create whatever we need to have a better future, there is an inherent risk of becoming a worker bee. Not a bad thing, but balance is required, or we can slip back into the scarcity perspective of a workaholic. When we believe the power to create financial stability lies solely within our capacity to create money, it's easy to fall into the trap of working harder and harder to create more and more. This is the dark side of moderate abundance.

Yes, this perspective does somewhat resemble the second scarcity money theme: *I must work hard and be responsible*. Remember, we're in the moderate zone, so there's still a tendency to slide back into scarcity as situations arise and change. The difference in this subcategory is that the worker bee knows, without equivocation, that he has the ability to earn the money he needs for a better future, the key word being *earn*. Worker bees assume financial responsibility whereas in the money theme of scarcity, financial responsibility is either nonexistent or viewed as burdensome. Entrepreneurs can easily fall into the worker bee category if they are resourceful enough.

As we unfold the nuances between scarcity and abundance, it should be easy to see the importance of mindset. We can easily engage in the very same acts of earning, spending, and saving. The difference is in how we perceive and experience those acts and the emotions that either enhance or inhibit our propensity for abundance.

In this specific perspective, the good news is that the worker bee enjoys the work he does, and he has no problem placing a value on his time. In other words, compensation is equal to perceived value of the work. Money is viewed as an exchange for goods and services. Here again, we see a stark contrast from High-to-Moderate Money Scarcity because in the two sub-perspectives of scarcity, people either have difficulty asking for compensation at all or they work hard and don't earn enough—often because they don't believe they deserve it.

Given this contrast, it's understandable that the worker bee experiences a completely different set of emotions in relation to money. Emotions of satisfaction, happiness, balance, and fulfillment are not uncommon. These individuals have the ability to earn what they need, and they value money but are not controlled by it. They pride themselves on having a great work ethic, and they may earn, spend, and save wisely. This sense of responsibility may also cause them to delay immediate self-gratification in favor of long-term purchases, e.g., saving for a home or car.

Even though the worker bee essentially knows that he has the capacity to earn the money needed, the worker bee may not be totally convinced that what he earns will be enough. Hence, the category of Moderate Money Abundance indicates a propensity to hold on to some level of scarcity because, after all, financial security is important. Even so, the worker bee enjoys a healthy balance between work and play, plans and saves for the future, and, generally speaking, practices good stewardship by avoiding unnecessary debt. Additionally, the worker bee will seek wise counsel to ensure that all resources are properly protected and secured.

Because the worker bee understands the flow of money, however, he does not hold on tightly. The worker bee is able to let go as situations arise and change and, similar to the earlier example of my client Barry, start up and begin again. This level of moderate abundance, then, encompasses a certain level of resiliency.

Perspective No. 2: The Selective Giver

In the moderate storyline of abundance, generosity begins to shift away from the fear of not having enough for self and others. The Selective Giver believes that money should be earned, budgeted, saved, and shared with those in need. This level of generosity, however, will depend on where the person falls in the spectrum of earning. In other words, The Selective Giver will give according to what is convenient to her own lifestyle.

The Selective Giver has a desire to share resources with others, but because she stands on the precipice between scarcity and abundance, it may still be somewhat difficult to freely give without worry or concern of having enough to meet her own need for comfort. This level of generosity may stem from a deep sense of responsibility to give or even from a need for approval. In other words, there is still an egocentric level of giving that does not allow for the freedom often associated with stewardship and an abundant spirit of generosity.

The Selective Giver generally gives as long as it's convenient to do so. The nuances of generosity are particularly interesting as we shift from High Scarcity to Moderate Abundance because the outcomes can look the same.[6] If we attempt to tease out the differences between these two levels of generosity, the main differences lie in the subtle distinctions between fear and responsibility.

For instance, people who indicate Forced Generosity in the category of Moderate Scarcity might only indicate acts of generosity with very small contributions or on rare occasions. Fear would be the emotion underlying the decision of what to give and how often: "What if I run out of financial resources, and I can't pay my bills?"

---

6   Appendix A indicates the contrast between the moderate scarcity perspective of Forced Generosity and the moderate abundance perspective of Selective Giver.

In the Moderate Abundance category, however, a person might be more inclined to give more money, more often, and to specific people or charities that the person cares about or deems important. This level of giving is based on a sense of responsibility to others, however, as stated above, it may even be clouded by a need to look good in the eyes of many. Giving might also be restricted to immediate family or friends. The conversation in this scenario might then be: "I'll give a specific amount because I know I can generate more, but I'll not give to the point of sacrificing my own wants and desires."

As you may have probably noticed, it's not always easy to differentiate scarcity from abundance. The outcomes can often look the same particularly when we're looking at generosity.

High Abundance Money Storyline #2: *I have the ability to create the money I need and share my resources with others.*
This second storyline of High Money Abundance represents a giant shift in perspective. Here, we move from *the capacity to earn* to *the ability to create*. This seemingly subtle distinction is huge in that the "capacity to earn" might fluctuate and change, for instance, if I lose the security of my job or position. Believing in the "ability to create," however, is significant because this perspective supports an internal understanding that I have control over my earnings regardless of external circumstances. Entrepreneurs with healthy and robust perspectives often fall into this category because they firmly believe in their abilities to "create" the financial resources they need.

The abundant perspective, then, is less about a capability and what you can do. Rather, it represents a way of *being*.

My research indicates that people with this perspective have, for the most part, freedom from the bondage of worry, stress, guilt, fear, frustration, and anxiety. This is not to say that they don't experience any negative emotions. Life circumstances wax and wane, and the flow of money in our lives changes. However, people who fall into this category can hold their emotions in perspective without being held captive by them. They are more prepared to adapt to life challenges. Even when they do experience the highs and lows of money, they use those circumstances and the emotions associated with them as jumping-off points or as sources of creative energy to spearhead them into the next phase of earning.

Here again, this storyline that abundant thinkers demonstrate is often separate and apart from how much money they have or don't have. This is why we often hear about entrepreneurs who have acquired large sums of wealth, lost it, and acquired it again and again.

This level of creative resilience is not without effort. It does, however, include a certain "love of the game" for the sake of the game. People who live from this high level of abundance express emotions of joy and contentment. They are often content with their financial circumstances even when they fluctuate and change, and their creativity often encompasses a heart and mind of generosity.

In essence, they are prepared for whatever external circumstances come their way because

- they understand the flow of money at the highest level;
- their identity is not dependent on their possessions;
- they are confident in their ability to create financial resources no matter what else is going on in the world; and
- they are stewards of those financial resources.

Within this storyline of High Abundance, let's examine two additional key perspectives that are showing up in my research. Here again, I'll ask that you consider how these perspectives may be affecting your own personal or professional life and if there is work to be done that will help you shift into more positive outcomes with respect to money.

Perspective No. 1: The Flow of Money

This perspective involves a positive belief with regard to the flow of money: *I proactively create the flow rather than react to it*. Similar to those who fall into the Moderate Abundance mindset, people who fall within the High Abundance range indicate early-childhood storylines that may set the stage for hard work and a desire to save and spend wisely. People in this category may also believe that money should be earned based on effort and that it should not be wasted on frivolity.

The difference, however, is that the definition of "frivolous" differs from the earlier ranges in that an abundant perspective also includes an appreciation for a balanced lifestyle. The need for money extends, then, beyond basic needs to include fun and recreation. Fully embodying the creative flow of money allows a person to work and play equally hard. People with this perspective may also have a greater tendency to spend money on luxury items, vacations, cars, and such, because they believe they deserve to reap the benefits of their hard-earned money. They are able to do so without guilt, shame, or worry.

This being said, however, people who live from abundance are not hedonists; they do not live beyond their means because they also understand that abundance includes a higher level of responsibility. For them, responsibility is different from the burden of responsibility mentioned in the earlier ranges. People who operate from abundance understand responsibility as opportunity—the opportunity to contribute beyond their own basic wants and needs to the greater good of society. This responsibility equates to a sophisticated level of stewardship as described in chapter 10.

Think Warren Buffet or Bill Gates. Yes, it's easy to think that they proactively respond to the flow of money because they're billionaires.

Remember, however, that they were not always this wealthy, and even in their wealth, they appear to embody abundant perspectives that are realized via philanthropic efforts and a commitment to the greater good of society.

As we once again try to contrast the subtleties between Moderate-to-High levels of money abundance, it might be helpful to think of the shift in this way: The shift goes from "me and mine" to "mine and yours." This shift is most obvious in how acts of generosity are played out.

Perspective No. 2: The Generous Giver

Within this perspective, we find a worldview that extends well beyond that of the Selective Giver. In this way of being: *I give from the heart and look for ways to contribute to the greater good.* If we quickly review the progression from High Money Scarcity to High Money Abundance as expressed in the Potential for Generosity framework in Appendix A, we will see a range that moves from Lack of Generosity, to Forced Generosity, to Selective Generosity, to the final abundant category of the Generous Heart. This heart is lived out by way of the Generous Giver in significant ways. This level of giving is a deep-felt desire to contribute to the well-being of others, and it is separate and apart from any dysfunctional need to be noticed, liked, or loved.

The Generous Giver comes from a deep and abiding joy in giving. Yes, money still offers a level of safety and security. Yes, money is deemed necessary to function in society and utilized to meet basic and desired needs. However, the Generous Giver embodies stewardship such that he is able to share acquired resources for the benefit of society.

Remember, the essence of abundance is that there are enough resources for everyone—even enough to share.

If you are a Generous Giver, you are most likely very intentional about how you share your resources. Once a greater cause tugs at your heart and is decided upon, you are loyal and consistent in your giving. You might even sacrifice your own wants and needs in order to give. This level of abundant thought is embedded in a place of gratitude and appreciation for all you have. This perspective translates into how you live out your experience with money. The premise of stewardship has deepened your experience of money in that you no longer chase the dollar. Rather, money flows toward you, and you are open to receive it and even more willing to share it.

Reflective Practice:
Part IV addresses what is required to shift your paradigms from scarcity to abundance.

Chapter 11 is designed to help you explore where you fall on the spectrum of Moderate-to-High levels of abundant thinking with respect to *money*. In this practice, you will explore your own *potential for generosity* and the subtle nuances between the Selective Giver and the Generous Giver. Review the Potential for Generosity categories in Appendix A. Spend some time reflecting on where you might fall in this spectrum of generosity. Pay special attention to the work yet to be done in order to transform your perspective on generosity to one that embodies abundance.

Then, spend at least 30 minutes journaling your responses to the following questions:

- Where do you categorize yourself on the spectrum of generosity?
- Give some examples of how this level of generosity plays out in your everyday life?
- What specific things might you do differently to shift to the perspective of a Generous Giver?
- How will you know when you get there?

12

A New Perspective on Time

I n their groundbreaking work on time, authors Zimbardo and Boyd offer a beautiful example of why time matters. Succinctly stated, it matters because time is finite.[67] We have only so much time in one lifetime. Additionally, our perspectives on time impact the decisions we make and ultimately the lives we lead. They also agree that our perspectives on time are learned and that we have the potential to change those perspectives.[68]

Let's now explore this potential for change by examining the time storylines associated with Moderate-to-High Abundance. The Outward Expressions associated with Moderate Time Abundance center around a sense of focus, an appreciation for flexibility, rest, and relaxation, a belief of control over one's own time, and the perception of a balanced lifestyle.

Who among us does not crave these very things? Yet, even within the moderate category of abundance, time can be experienced in somewhat negative ways as is evidenced by this first storyline.

Moderate Time Abundance Storyline #1:
Time is fleeting; I should manage it well.

A perspective of Moderate Abundance with respect to time indicates a capable stance. People who fall into this category may experience less stress and fewer negative emotions about time because they view time as a commodity that should be managed and used wisely.

As the storyline indicates, people with this worldview don't have a need to chase time. They do, however, value it enough to use it with discretion. Time is experienced as a continuum that marks the passing of events, so they appreciate flexibility and having control over their own schedules. When they make time for family and recreation, it's far easier for them to be present in the moment because they are good at prioritizing their time. Because it's important for these individuals to avoid feelings of stress or hurry, they are very considerate of other people's time. They are rarely late for events or appointments.

In contrast to a scarcity perspective on time, a sense of time as fleeting helps to keep people with this storyline energized and focused. People who share in this perspective may have a great sense of accomplishment at the end of each day. They are confident in their abilities to meet their goals and objectives irrespective of what the clock may dictate.

Within this first storyline of Moderate Abundance, let's examine a few key perspectives that people may have in relation to their experience of time.

Perspective No. 1: Control Over Time

People who enjoy this perspective balance the fulcrum between scarcity and abundance of time. They are adept at balancing their time between work and family. What this means is that their need and ability to control or manage time works in their favor because it helps them produce results.

This need, however, can also work against them if they begin to take on too much. Overconfidence in their ability to control their schedule might cause them to slip into feelings of scarcity. For example, if they get overloaded with work, they may also feel overwhelmed by family responsibilities. Because they value moments with family, they can usually sort these moments out. If, however, they begin to feel a need for strong control over their time, it may be an indicator that they are regressing to scarcity perspectives.

From a perspective of Moderate Abundance, this sense of control keeps people focused and fluid to whatever needs to happen throughout the day. They may pride themselves on their ability to multitask and prioritize throughout the day and week. The ability to prioritize time enables them to avoid an obsessive need for control. Such individuals may have a tendency to be on time; however, this tendency may cause them to be critical of others who do not value time in the same way.

Within this perspective, time is also viewed as "fleeting." The question then becomes how to prioritize and still maintain a sense of control over time that is not rigid or overwhelming. This balanced sense of control, for the most part, allows for the capacity to address priorities as they arise to include a keen sense of what's important on the home front as well as in the office.

Additionally, the sense of control over one's own time also allows space for Intentional Generosity of time as depicted in Appendix B. In other words, this theme supports the premise: I must be willing to work hard, but I must never lose site of the reality that time is fleeting. I must control my time so as to allow ample time for the people I love.

Perspective No. 2: Sense of Accomplishment

People in this subcategory have a sense of accomplishment at the end of each day, and this sense is not necessarily directly linked to how much they actually get done. The mantra here might be expressed in this way: *I always feel like I've had a productive day even when things are left for tomorrow.* Such individuals have the ability to prioritize and balance their need for control over time because they do not set unrealistic expectations for their day.

Because time is viewed as a continuum that marks the passing of events, people who live from this worldview do not experience a sense of failure or overwhelm if they don't get everything done as they'd hoped. Even when the day gets harried and filled with unexpected activities, they have the ability to flow with the most important priorities and feel good about whatever they accomplish. Whatever doesn't get done today will move to the top of the list for tomorrow.

This sense of accomplishment stems directly from an ability to shift and move tasks, responsibilities, and focus in the direction needed. The added bonus lies in thoughts, feelings, and emotions of joy, fulfillment, and high levels of self-efficacy. Such manifestations of abundance in turn create a cycle of accomplishment. Even in the midst of deadlines and shortages of time, this sense of accomplishment serves as ongoing proof: I can make things happen no matter the time limitations of my day or week.

This worldview, if carefully monitored, further positions a person to eventually move into High Time Abundance perspectives as evidenced in the second storyline.

High Time Abundance Storyline #2:
Time is a precious resource; I enjoy every moment.

This perspective shifts a person's "management" of time to a place of "being" in the moment. Herein lies a subtle distinction of having enough time to accomplish whatever you want whenever you want. Time is precious, and it is used wisely. The difference here is that such individuals respect both the concrete and the abstract nature of time. Time, you see, is a precious treasure. Time is not simply managed in the name of "getting more things done." Time is valued and respected because it is recognized as finite. The most valuable thing a person can do is spend time with family and loved ones. Family, for these individuals, undoubtedly comes first.

Within this storyline, the thoughts, feelings, emotions, or perceptions about time center on a sense of control not only over time but of one's own life. There is, therefore, freedom to choose how your time is utilized. People who fall within this storyline speak to being fully present in the daily moments of their lives. They express feelings of gratitude and joy for *every* moment, and they are free from guilt when they relax or take time for loved ones. Every moment is precious.

Because family comes first for these individuals, people who live from this perspective will rarely sacrifice those precious moments for work-related deadlines. They will get the job done, but they will often work around the needs of those they cherish most. This is particularly important to know if you somehow find yourself in a work environment that does not value or respect your need for personal time or your ability to balance work and family.

The ability to prioritize goes beyond capability in this storyline. There is more of a proactive stance that allows the individual to put first things first. Because of the ability to balance work and family, these individuals rarely experience the negative emotions associated with scarcity of time. When they are at work, they are fully present. By the same token, when they take time out for family, they are rarely thinking about deadlines or having guilt or regret for not being at work.

Time is valued and respected. Within this framework, two additional perspectives emerge.

Perspective No. 1: Family as Priority

People with a high sense of abundance come from the worldview that family comes before everything else—even more money. One of the leaders I interviewed in my research, for example, boldly walked away from career opportunities that would have separated him from his family. What we see here is less about the act of balancing than it is about the principle of family first. Such overt actions are rarely necessary, however, because with this high sense of having enough time to do it all, the abundant perspective allows for a higher sense of creativity that may ultimately result in the family being involved in work.

For instance, people who live from this perspective enjoy a Generous Spirit when it comes to how they utilize their time. For example, they might find ways to include their families on extended business trips. If they operate in entrepreneurial environments, they might pay their teenagers to work within their businesses. It's not about how much time they spend with family or how much time they spend working. The point is that they live from a perspective that family takes precedence over work. This level of abundant thinking then leads to creative solutions that are less emotionally stressful.

Here again, we see the ability to experience time at both the concrete and abstract levels. In other words, people who live from this perspective have the ability to honor the ticking clock but not be ruled by it. Family coming first is not just jargon or lip service. Such individuals do not just go through the daily responsible tasks required for caring and providing for a family. They are intentional in how they spend time with family or loved ones. Play and recreation are vital to who they are. While the moderate perspective on time may generate a need to schedule such activities, people who live from high abundance may be freely open to moments of play as a natural part of how they live out their daily lives.

Play often equates to greater presence and the ability to respond to opportunities for joy as they arise. A pure sense of task-orientation might look like putting your children to bed at night whereas "play" would incorporate taking the additional time to read them a bedtime story. Perhaps even laughing and talking about that story beyond the designated bedtime. Such moments are never taken for granted. Viewing time as precious allows for gratitude and joy in the moment. Additionally, time with family and loved ones goes well beyond the task or a sense of responsibility. Time is about making memories and enjoying every moment with those you care about.

Perspective No. 2: The Compass of Positive Emotions
In this perspective, we find people who pay attention to their positive emotions, and when they witness themselves slipping into scarcity or fear, they self-correct accordingly. They do not wait for crisis to arrive on the scene. This stance allows for more intentional use of self. People who live from this perspective often speak to a heightened awareness of their emotions. They are directors of their own movie.

The good news for people who share this perspective is that they don't have much tolerance for negative emotions in their daily lives. When they do slip into feelings of being overwhelmed or frustrated, it feels like quicksand because they're not used to living out of such felt scarcity. If abundant thinking produces positive emotions, moments of negativity are more pronounced and obvious. They are examined and dealt with quickly.

This heightened level of awareness is also important to overall health and well-being and should be respected. If you fall within this range, there's a good chance that you have the capacity to pull yourself out of situations that may cause you to experience negative emotions of guilt, shame, fear, anxiety, or any sense of feeling overwhelmed and frustrated, and you can willfully do so with far greater ease than someone who lives from the norm of scarcity. Value your abundant perspective and guard against those who might attempt to engage you in the perspective that there is never enough time to be all that you want or need to be.

Within this context of High Abundance, there is also a tendency to "live with no regrets," so every moment of every day is intentional even as it is free-flowing and open to new possibilities for connection with others.

Reflective Practice:

Chapter 12 focuses on Moderate-to-High levels of abundant thinking with respect to *time*. Within this context, this reflective practice will focus on your *self-efficacy* with respect to time as outlined in Appendix B. Self-efficacy can be defined as "beliefs in one's capabilities to organize and execute the course of action required to produce given [results].[69] This reflective practice then will ask you to explore what supports you most in having a sense of control over your own time.

Review the points on Appendix B with respect to Moderate-to-High level of abundance and self-efficacy. Rate yourself on a scale of 1-5 on each point. Select one area you want to focus on in order to attain greater self-efficacy. Spend a minimum of two weeks taking action in this area. Then, journal responses to the following questions:

- What one specific element of abundance did you focus on to help you achieve self-efficacy with respect to time?
- What actions did you take to help you move in this direction?
- What outcomes did you experience?
- How did this practice help you move closer to a high abundant perspective on time?

13

THE SECRET TO A
MEANINGFUL, PROSPEROUS LIFE

E arlier, I briefly alluded to the practice of stewardship as the secret, most important way to live out a meaningful, prosperous life. In this chapter, I'll show you how to develop a practice of stewardship as one way to achieve this goal, but first, please take a brief moment to imagine how different your life might be if you could implement every concept and every Reflective Practice we've explored thus far. Can you imagine yourself experiencing the existing chase for time and money differently–from a true spirit of abundance? Do you think you might have a healthier more robust experience of life? What we have essentially been talking about is a bigger life, one free from all those negative thoughts and emotions that have been plaguing you whenever you're forced to deal with time and money.

I've talked about the potential for your early-childhood stories to impact your current way of thinking about time and money. I've indicated that there is often a relationship between time and money and if you're chasing one, you're most likely chasing the other. I've also suggested that the abstract and concrete dual-nature of time and money adds to the complexity we face each and every day as we attempt to accumulate, manage, and hold on to these two most important resources. I've even stated that these resources, while vital to how we live out our daily experience of life, are an opportunity to go beyond practicality to a place where we recognize time and money as a window into our very soul.

I have also defined stewardship as a practice that could set you on a path to a more abundant experience with time and money. Let's now go a bit deeper into specific ways that you can enhance this practice so that you can more fully discover the secret to a meaningful and prosperous life.

Stewardship is the key to setting us free. When we fully embody stewardship, we shift our thoughts and actions to a place where time and money no longer control us. Rather, we grow into mastery over time and money, and we do so from a healthy, integrated place. And, once again, the added benefit of stewardship is that it has nothing to do with how much or how little time and money we actually have.

Remember, stewardship is a mindset that encompasses our individual responsibility to use our resources wisely. This level of responsibility involves an abundant spirit of healthy generosity and service to others. We honor our work and family commitments as we are simultaneously open to what is best for the greater good of humanity. Our commitment to goodness overrides our own egocentric desires.

Stewardship produces a meaningful and prosperous life. Prosperity, then, is something far greater than the accumulation of wealth and three fancy cars in the garage. Prosperity is fueled by stewardship. It is a way of life. In practical terms, this way of thinking, doing, and being acts as a cycle, which I will address more fully in Chapter 14. For now, let's examine some basic premises associated with the practice of stewardship.

A Scientific Approach to Stewardship

In previous chapters, I have offered up a brief overview of the distinctions between states, stages, and lines of development. I also stated that there is evidence to support that we experience the concrete and abstract nature of time and money, at least to some degree, based on our state, stage of adult development, and capacities within each line of development. These are complex dimensions of who we are as human beings. From a human developmental perspective, two research-based frameworks help us to wrap our minds around this complexity. We can explore our thoughts and behaviors in the context of Integral Theory and the AQAL Model.[70]

Integral theory is the most inclusive and theoretically sound theory of our time because it explores multiple patterns of reality across all major disciplines, e.g., the arts and humanities, the social sciences, religion, law, health care, economics, to include many other disciplines and forms of knowledge.[71]

Integral theory also helps us understand human developmental stages, states, and lines. It supports a comprehensive exploration into how we currently think and behave in relation to life and to our experience of time and money. It also points us to where we might need to develop additional competencies related to stewardship.

The theory was created by American philosopher Ken Wilber in the 1970s with the release of his first book, *The Spectrum of Consciousness*.[72] This groundbreaking work led Wilber to explore and write about various major disciplines in the context of integral theory over the course of thirty-seven years. Today, Wilber's collected works have been translated into over 24 languages, and integral theory is used globally in over 35 academic and professional fields.[73]

The theory, in all its complexity, is beyond the scope of this book. We can, however, access this theory via Wilber's AQAL Model. This model allows us expand our earlier discussion on the stages and lines of development in that it serves as a map that can guide us through the territory of our own awareness in relation to time, money, and stewardship.[74]

As scholar Sean Esbjorn-Hargens[75] explained:

[The AQAL Model] is a *framework* because it creates a mental space where one can organize and index their and others' current activities in a clear and coherent manner. It is a *theory* because it offers an explanation for how the most time-tested methodologies and data they generate can fit together. It is a *practice* because it is not just a theory about inclusion but an actual series of practices of inclusion . . . the AQAL model can be summarized as a third-person map of reality, a second-person framework for working within and across disciplines, and a first-person practice for engaging the development of our own embodied awareness.[76]

As is evidenced by this quote, the AQAL Model affords us the perfect opportunity to not only explore our thoughts and behaviors in relation to time and money. It also creates space for us to explore new practices associated with stewardship.

Utilizing the four quadrants of the model as an integral lens, we can, therefore, explore practices of stewardship in relation to our use of time and money. Figure 1 demonstrates a visual overview that is representative of this most basic form of the model.

Figure 1

An Integral Approach to Time, Money, and Stewardship

	Interior	Exterior
Individual	**UL: How I *think* about my time and money.** • What are my beliefs about time? About money? • What are my personal values about time and money? • What emotions, thoughts, or feelings arise in me when I think about time? About money? • How do I determine if I have enough time and money? • If I had unlimited time and money, what would I do with it? • What do I believe to be important about time and money?	**UR: What I *do* with my time and money.** • Where is my time and money currently spent? • What outcomes are achieved as a result of this? • What is accomplished by my time and money? • How do my actions reflect my values about time and money? • What would I like to do with my time and money that I'm not currently dong? • How does my time and money contribute to my overall well-being and health? • What do I do, or not do, with my time and money?
Collective	**LL: How I *experience* my time and money in relation to others?** • What impact do I want to have on others through my use of time and money? • How do I currently collaborate on collective projects that require my time and money? • What collective outcomes or contributions are made as a result of my time and money? • How do I determine where my time and money is spent or invested? • Who helps or supports me in how I manage my time and money?	**LR: How I *plan* for my use of time and money?** • What frameworks are in place for long-term planning of my time and money? • How to I examine and measure outcomes with respect to my use of time and money? • What patterns do I see that are satisfactory with respect to how I utilize my time and money? • What may need to change? • To what degree do I contribute my time and money to help solve local and global problems?

©Spano (2016)   Adapted with permission from Integral Coaching Canada, Inc. (2013)

Before I describe how you can use the AQAL Model to explore your own experience of time and money, let me first offer a brief overview of what the four quadrants represent.

On the vertical axis, the AQAL quadrants are expressed in terms of interior and exterior[77] constructs whereas the horizontal axis represents linkage between the individual and the collective aspects of our world. It's important to note that while the quadrants can only be described in this one way, there are many ways to define each quadrant within the construct of the aspect we are considering. For purposes of this work, we are considering how one might experience time and money in the context of stewardship.

For example, we can address the relevancy of the quadrants by their location in relation to an individual's experience of time and money versus that of the collective. Or, we might consider an internal versus an external perspective, or the subjective versus the objective. In reviewing figure 1, the upper-left and upper-right quadrants, for example, represent the individual "I" or "It" space whereas the lower-left and lower-right quadrants represent the "We" and "Its" space. An integral approach to how we manage and utilize our time and money would suggest that we consider our perspectives from all four quadrants. Additionally, our perspectives are uniquely linked to one or two primary quadrants.[78] Even so, any predominant perspectives from any one of the quadrants co-arises and informs the others. Ken Wilber would remind us—each perspective is partial and true.

Before I explain how you can utilize this model to determine where you land in relation to stewardship, allow me to offer up an example. Remember, we are considering the AQAL Model as a map, so the point here is to explore where you might land on this map. The territory of the map includes the elements expressed above, e.g., individual, collective, interior, exterior. Additionally, a more complex rendition of this framework would also include the stages, states, and lines of human development[79] as we have been discussing them.

One quadrant is not better than another. Only different. If, however, I come to notice that I have certain patterns arise in one quadrant over another with respect to this specific topic of stewardship, I might consider additional practices relative to the other quadrants. Doing so will help me transition to more abundant thought with respect to my experience of time, money, and any potential for stewardship. I have designed figure 1 for just this reason: to help you increase awareness in these specific areas.

I'm going to suggest a Reflective Practice in this chapter that allows you to explore the questions in figure 1. Before I do, however, let me offer a concrete example of how such exploration might lead you to a heightened awareness about your experience of time and money.

Let's imagine, for example, that I journal specific responses to all of the questions in figure 1. Depending on my scores for the journal responses in the upper-left quadrant, I might begin to notice a pattern of beliefs about time and money. Stewardship might come into play as I recognize patterns of thoughts and behaviors that embody all four quadrants in ways that support my having a meaningful and prosperous life. For instance, I might begin to notice patterns in the upper-right quadrant that indicate specific ways in which I spend my time and money in order to maintain a healthy body. Or, I might begin to see that I do a fairly good job of contributing my time and money to others (the lower-left quadrant). I might be equally concerned about contributing in ways that help to solve local and global problems (lower-right quadrant).

Given my responses and the patterns I see, I will come to notice that I have very specific ways of being with respect to my use of time and money. If I hold a conditional belief that my time and money are to be used for the greater good of others, can you imagine how I might think and feel if I shift over into the upper-right quadrant and choose to *behave* in frivolous ways? A shoe-shopping spree, for example, might cause me to slide into guilt and shame. I might not feel that my time and money were utilized well because the shopping spree did not align with my interior perspectives on time and money. Essentially, I'm working against my own sense of well-being.

It's equally important to remember that we're not attempting to box ourselves into one quadrant or another as each impacts the other and the point is that we want an integrated approach to stewardship that allows us to *think, do, experience,* and *plan* how we utilize our time and money from all four quadrants. The questions are merely tools to help you explore your own awareness. Each of us will have different responses to the same questions.

Let's explore another simplified example. If I look to the questions in the upper-left quadrant and find myself *thinking* about my time and money, in whatever form, but I fail to *experience* it in relation to others, e.g., I have trouble contributing or giving of my time and money, I may find myself slipping into scarcity elements of emptiness or even isolation. Or, if I'm frivolously spending (upper-right) all the time with little room to *plan* (lower-right) for my future, I may be heading for disaster. And so it goes.

We can explore each of the questions from multiple perspectives and come up with a different scenario each and every time. And, that is exactly the point—to explore the questions in the context of who you are and how you *think, do, experience,* and *plan* your use of time and money. Your responses to the questions in the quadrants will grant you greater awareness with respect to your unique perspectives and your potential for acts of stewardship.

In chapter 10, I stated that stewardship encompasses our capacity to use our individual resources wisely, and this includes a healthy sense of generosity and a willingness to serve others. As a first step into stewardship, I invite you to spend some reflective time with figure 1 and explore the AQAL Model in relation to your use of time and money as you experience it right *now* in your life. Not as you hope to be someday, but as you are right now. Understanding your current way of being is important to your future development, so please trust and enjoy the process as described in the Reflective Practice segment of this chapter.

Reflective Practice

Chapter 13 focuses on helping you develop an *integral perspective* on your experience of time and money. Using the questions represented in the AQAL Model will help you begin to discover patterns of thought and behavior in relation to your experience of time, money, and stewardship. In discovering these patterns of thought and behavior, you move one step closer to stewardship and the prospect of a meaningful prosperous life.

Over the next four days, spend time journaling your responses to only one of the four quadrants in figure 1. Please do not rush this process. Give yourself time to reflect in an open and honest way. There are no right or wrong answers. Your responses should be reflective of your life as it stands right now. Not as you wish it to be.

Once you have all your responses completed for each question, review those responses using the following scale to help you determine how often the elements of your responses are present in the here and now:

0 = Not at all present
1 = Rarely present
2 = Infrequently present
3 = Somewhat present
4 = Mostly present
5 = Totally present

For example, if you have a response in the lower left quadrant that indicates that you currently collaborate on collective projects that require your time and money, how well or how often do you do this? If your answer is often, then you might give yourself a 5. If you notice that you rarely collaborate in this way, you might then give yourself a 2. Once you have answered the questions in figure 1, completed your journaling, and scored your responses accordingly, journal responses to the following questions:

- What patterns did you notice with respect to time? Money?
- Did responses in one quadrant indicate more of an abundant perspective on time and money than another?
- What's one specific area that you'd like to have more fully present in your life?
- What one specific area would help you more fully embody stewardship as a way of life?

14

LIVING IN THE CYCLE OF FREEDOM™

I briefly mentioned this Cycle of Freedom™ earlier. Now that we have explored some important ideas that will help you shift from scarcity to abundance and what it can mean to live a life of stewardship and greater prosperity, let's take a deeper dive into what that Cycle of Freedom™ looks like and how it can support your continued practice of stewardship and personal and professional growth.

Although the virtues I'm describing in the Cycle of Freedom™ do not necessarily flow in a linear path from one to another, research indicates that each is beneficial to our overall well-being. As you review this cycle, bear in mind, that generosity, gratitude, compassion, and love are abstract, complex ideas that have been studied and researched in theological, philosophical, and more recently, psychological circles for thousands of years. Utilizing the Integral Approach to Time, Money, and

Figure 2: Time and Money Cycle of Freedom©

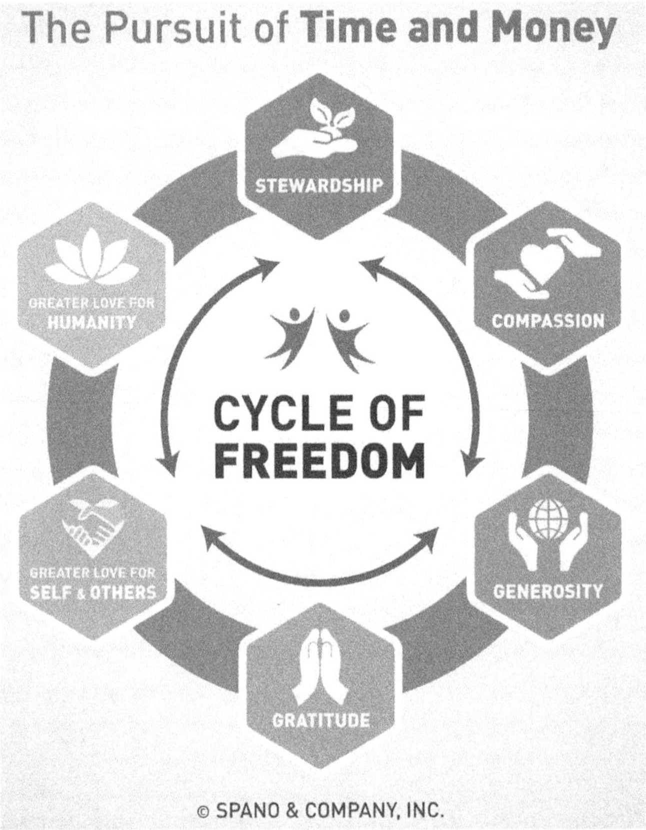

The Pursuit of **Time and Money**

STEWARDSHIP

GREATER LOVE FOR HUMANITY

COMPASSION

CYCLE OF FREEDOM

GREATER LOVE FOR SELF & OTHERS

GENEROSITY

GRATITUDE

© SPANO & COMPANY, INC.

Stewardship© as depicted in figure 1, you can explore how to embrace these virtues in more specific ways.

The underlying goal here is to help you come to some deeper understanding about the potential for a meaningful, prosperous life—a bigger life. Remember, the goal of a healthy and robust approach to how you utilize your time and money can be achieved at every developmental level. Consideration of the attitudes and behaviors you might adopt in relation to the Cycle of Freedom™ can help you move in that direction.

Now, let's briefly unfold the virtues associated with the Cycle of Freedom™. Remember, we're speaking to these virtues as outcomes of stewardship. The goal might be, for instance, to live out an integral perspective of stewardship utilizing all four quadrants in figure 1 from the previous chapter such that you embrace these virtues.

Generosity

Generosity is an outcome of stewardship. Generosity absent stewardship, however, shows up as an imposter of abundance. Remember, the narcissistic generosity I referred to in my example of King Henry VIII in chapter 5? Pathological generosities that are egocentric and destructive can and do arise. Researcher Akhtar contends that generosity is a trait linked to early child development and that "generosity toward and from others remains a lifelong partner of psychic development and stability."[80] When we do not develop in appropriate ways, e.g., absent the care and love of a mother, we are more susceptible to pathological generosities.[81]

It is important, therefore, to examine our potential for generosity if we are to embrace a meaningful, prosperous life. This is precisely why I began this work with a glimpse into early-childhood stories. The point, once again, is not to make anyone wrong or to blame another for how we live out our experience of time and money. The point is to develop awareness of what is working for or against us so that we can improve our chances for a bigger life.

Moving beyond any tendency for pathological "giving," let's focus more specifically on the healthier side of generosity. Researcher Deprose expands the trait of generosity beyond an exchange of good, services, and possessions to include an openness to others that undercuts any propensity for a self-contained ego. She further describes generosity as an "openness to others that is fundamental to human existence, sociality, and social formation."[82]

Generosity is vital to our very health and well-being. It has the potential to shift our relationship with time and money. The subtle nuances between scarcity and abundance with respect to generosity as depicted in Appendices A and B suggest that our lived experience of generosity with respect to time can range from a total Lack of Generosity to a Generous Spirit that allows us to live more freely in the moment and to enjoy time with loved ones. In the context of money, authentic generosity extends beyond the act of material gifts to matters of the heart and mind. Generosity dictates that we accept people for who they are and that we appreciate their perspectives alongside our own. In this context, the disparity is even more obvious ranging from an inability to give to others at all across the spectrum to include a generous heart that contributes to the greater good of society.

If we think back to our earlier discussion on stages of development and the AQAL Model, the point is not to make ourselves wrong or feel guilty or ashamed about our level of generosity. Such negative expressions only serve to compound the matter. The point is to simply note where you stand on the spectrum of generosity such that you can make reasonable changes. As we come to embrace more abundant perspectives and take on the task of stewardship, generosity will unfold. And with it, a greater sense of gratitude which brings us to the next virtue on the Cycle of Freedom.™

Gratitude

Gratitude is "the quality of being thankful; readiness to show appreciation for and to return kindness."[83] When we open up our hearts and minds to generosity and learn to contribute from a deeper level, we experience the gratitude of others and, in doing so, we ourselves become more grateful.

Gratitude is also a way to put things into perspective;[84] it's a way to improve our own lives and the lives of others. There is an underlying dynamic to gratitude in that the act of gratitude rests in the fact that goodness has come to us and it is goodness we give back. The "heart of the gratitude experience is best reflected, simply, by the phrase, *the giving away of goodness.*"[85] Because gratitude contributes to our sense of well-being and allows us to experience greater fulfillment and joy in life, it helps protect us from unrestrained wants and desires.[86]

Gratitude, then, affects our behavior and has the potential to impact how we utilize our time and money. Researcher Shelton goes on to suggest that acts of gratitude generate positive emotions. He further adds that gratitude is important to our growth and development, helps us to behave in more caring ways, and strengthens our relationships and ties to the wider community. More importantly, gratitude helps us experience the fullest expression of love.[87] I would add that all of these positive outcomes equip us to fight off the scarcity monsters of stress, worry, and fear.

So, is gratitude an emotion, a virtue, or a combination of both? Thought leaders from every discipline still grapple with the significance of gratitude. Gratitude can be experienced and expressed in many different forms. What we do know is that gratitude shapes our identity and is one of the building blocks of our society.[88] We also know that gratitude has a nature of duality. Some distinguish between a gratitude of exchange and a gratitude of caring.[89] Simply stated, gratitude can be described in the context of "the kind we feel for what we take and the larger kind we find for what we give."[90]

When we think, for example, about the basic exchange of time for money, we might find ourselves grateful for a paycheck. Or, not so grateful, depending on the amount of dollars earned in relation to our effort. However, in the context of the Cycle of Freedom™ and the underlying premise of prosperity, we are wise to consider the power underlying a gratitude of caring.

A gratitude of caring involves a personal relationship with another, one that may involve, or, more importantly, evolve to love and bonding at the core. This level of gratitude is linked to our sense of morality.[91] In this scenario, the economics of exchange do not apply. In a gratitude of caring, "Loving involves giving, and the greater the giving, the greater the benefit received by the giver."[92]

If we return once again to Appendices A and B, we can see how someone living from a scarcity perspective who struggles with the notion of generosity might have a more difficult time experiencing the benefits of gratitude. In order to break the cycle of fear and scarcity, stewardship is required. Stewardship always supports a gratitude of caring because with good stewardship, there is enough to give even when there isn't much at all.

And, to those who are able to embrace a larger perspective of generosity and gratitude comes the blessing of compassion.

Compassion

Dare I suggest that generosity absent a spirit of gratitude equates to worthless acts? The outcome of gratitude is greater compassion because the heart is awakened to the suffering of others. I, therefore, contend that gratitude evolves into a spirit of compassion. Compassion can be defined as the integration of feeling, mood, motivation, and actions—each poised toward the suffering of another. When we embody compassion, we have an ability to relate to the suffering of others and an even greater desire to alleviate that suffering.

Can you begin to imagine how this Cycle of Freedom™ builds toward better relationships and more love in our lives?

According to research authors Greenberg and Turksma, compassion is a core dimension of human nature that can be nurtured. When we nurture compassion within ourselves, we enjoy the express outcomes of personal growth, wellbeing, and life-enhancing relationships.[93] When we allow our pursuit of time and money to catapult us into scarcity and fear, we separate ourselves from our natural tendency for compassion. A scarcity survivor-mode mentality leaves little room for acts of compassion. On the other hand, when we demonstrate compassion via our utilization of our resources of time and money, our relationships grow in depth and meaning. Here again, our unsolicited reward is that we enhance our own propensity for greater health and well-being.[94] As an added bonus, acts of compassion even have the potential to alleviate the psychological stressors of frustration, anxiety, worry, and even depression.[95]

Another aspect of compassion that should not be overlooked has to do with our propensity for self-compassion. I find this premise to be particularly relevant to our discussion on stewardship because, let's face it, we make mistakes in how we spend our time and money. Remember, we flow in and out of our propensity for scarcity and abundance—all depending on our current circumstances.

If I've recently lost my job or squandered my paycheck, I'm going to experience more negative emotions in relation to my money and perhaps in relation to my time. As the circumstances change to less than positive scenarios, it's far easier for me to slide into self-deprecating thoughts and attitudes of blame: What was I thinking? What did I do to cause this to happen? I have failed my family! The thoughts go on and on often leading to cycles of guilt, shame, and, you guessed it, more fear and scarcity.

What I've witnessed in my practice is that leaders and business owners who have track records of success often fall into the trap of penalizing themselves for perceived failures. As our resources fluctuate and change—for whatever reason—it's vital that we learn coping mechanisms that allow for self-compassion. Failure to do so robs us of virtues associated with the Cycle of Freedom™. Rather, we become trapped by scarcity thoughts and behaviors that catapult us into defeat and despair.

Self-compassion is vital then to how we live out good stewardship. Stewardship will be difficult to embrace if we don't first embrace our own worthiness. When we foster self-compassion, failure becomes an opportunity to learn from our past mistakes. We are able to acknowledge that we are decent, worthy human beings, fully able to step into bigger lives.

Self-Compassion is basically comprised of three components:[96]

1. kindness toward oneself when facing pain or failure;
2. perceiving one's experiences as part of a larger human experience rather than feeling isolated; and
3. holding painful thoughts and feelings in balanced awareness.

Remember the example of fear and scarcity I offered up in chapter 5? David is one of many people I've experienced in my practice who was not able to give himself the gift of self-compassion. One perceived failure led to another and another. The result was a total lack of stewardship and an inability to fully experience the virtues associated with the Cycle of Freedom™. In short, David was in bondage to his past and his future, unable to break the cycle of scarcity that had plagued him for most of his life.

Contrast the example of David to that of Barry in chapter 11. Even as Barry was faced with an economic disaster that was well beyond his control, he understood that this situation was part of a bigger human experience. We could assume that he had moments of isolation, fear, and scarcity as anyone might under those conditions. However, the fact that he rose up from the ashes is an indicator that he was also able to hold any negative thoughts and feelings in perspective to what was going on in the global economy. This level of awareness and self-compassion resulted in his being able to recreate a new company and begin again.

As you reflect on the themes of scarcity discussed in chapters 5 and 6, it's important to consider that self-compassion has the potential to lead us toward more meaningful ways of using our time and money for the benefit of others. It also has the potential to increase self-compassion for ourselves when we slide into moments of fear and scarcity: When I believe myself worthy, and I'm willing to forget past stories and forgive my own mistakes, I can position myself for stewardship and more abundant perspectives on time and money.

The Cycle of Freedom and Experiencing Deeper Love and Belonging

The real power of the Cycle of Freedom™ is that, in addition to giving us a visual representation of the outcomes of stewardship, it also demonstrates how those outcomes can potentially bring us deeper senses of love and belonging in our personal and professional lives. Whether we realize it or not, our egocentric desires for power, control, or approval and any expression thereof, is really a deep, abiding search for more love in our life. This is why this cycle is so vital to our experience. When we consider our use of time and money as a window into the soul, we can embrace them as one avenue, albeit an important one, to how we love self, others, the greater society, and for those who are spiritually inclined, ultimately, God.

The Cycle of Freedom™ described as acts of stewardship accompanied by virtues of generosity, gratitude, and compassion ultimately positions us for enhanced well-being and greater love.

Reflective Practice:

Chapter 14 focuses on the *outcomes of stewardship*, namely, generosity, gratitude, and compassion as expressed in the Cycle of Freedom™. This practice is designed to help you reflect upon how you live out these outcomes. The point is to develop awareness of how your utilization of time and money translates into these various traits and virtues.

Designate a separate section in your journal for each of the virtues in The Cycle of Freedom™. Review the sections on each virtue, along with the Cycle of Freedom™ graphic, and determine one or two elements of that virtue that you would like to incorporate into your life. Feel free to come up with several of your own.

Once you've decided on the elements for each virtue that you want to incorporate into your life, focus on one virtue for a minimum of one week. Practice being the director of your own movie. Spend at least 15 minutes each evening journaling responses to the following questions:

- What element of which virtue did choose to focus on? Why?
- How did you live out that specific virtue?
- What patterns did you notice with respect to your capacity for stewardship via the virtues?
- What do you need to let go of in order to more fully embody stewardship?

15

LOVING FROM RADICAL ABUNDANCE

The truth —that love is the ultimate and the highest goal to which man can aspire . . . The salvation of man is through love and in love . . . a man who has nothing left in this world still may know bliss . . .
—from *Man's Search for Meaning* by Viktor E. Frankl

The Cycle of Freedom™ begins and ends with a deeper sense of love. If stewardship is the key to our time/money prison gate, and prosperity is what keeps that gate open, then love is the reason there's a gate in the first place. We are designed to love. We are the gateway to love, and that love begins with how well we love ourselves.

When we use our time and money in destructive ways, we fail to love ourselves well. The inability to love ourselves well translates into how well we love others and how well we contribute to the greater

165

good of society. Egocentric behaviors that are destructive and harmful, particularly in our use of time and money, destroy the gateway. All is lost. We chase time and money in unhealthy ways, and ultimately, we become enslaved by the dragon of fear and scarcity. We become the chase; we impose the chase on others.

The information I've shared with respect to various dimensions of self and adult human development can help you have a healthier experience of time and money. It can also help you shift to radical abundance such that you experience a more meaningful and prosperous life, one that includes deeper love for self and others. As we've seen from the many examples in this book, how we think about and utilize time and money is inextricably linked to our sense of love and belonging. When you learn to consistently practice good stewardship such that you fully experience the outcomes as described in the Cycle of Freedom™, you will experience radical abundance by way of a deeper love for yourself and for those around you.

In the preceding chapters, I laid out the relevance and importance of stages and lines of human development. One way to explore the path toward radical abundance is to evaluate where you currently land in terms of your own stage of development.[7] Additionally, I invite you to continue to reflect on your daily thoughts and feelings with respect to time and money and to ask yourself how your responses actually translate into *acts* of love.

For example, imagine a workaholic father who has little time for his children. If we go back to the Expert stage of development, we might see this man as a very good father. He is working hard to provide. He is not a bad person by any stretch of the imagination, but his view of parenting may be limited. In terms of his stage of human development,

---

7   If you are interested in knowing precisely where you fall on the spectrum of human development, please visit the work of Dr. Terri O'Fallon at *www. PacificIntegral.com.*

he is situated at one of the lower base camps we spoke about earlier. He's doing all he knows to do to make more money to secure a better financial future for his children. The only problem is he has absolutely no quality time for those children. Yes, he loves his children, but the deeper question is—do his children *feel* loved?

Engaging in a practice of stewardship will help that father develop healthier perspectives on time and money. Those healthier perspectives will readily equate to a different, but no less valid, pursuit of time and money. That different pursuit of time and money will perhaps afford him more quality time with his children. And that additional quality time will make his children *feel* more loved.

On the opposite end of the spectrum, imagine a boss who believes herself to be a responsible businessperson. Yet, her employees experience her as someone who ruthlessly drives them to work harder and harder often with little reward or proper remuneration. She drives a sleek, fancy car, takes amazing trips on holiday—all of which she has earned. Still, her employees believe themselves to be underappreciated and underpaid because she fails to demonstrate generosity, gratitude, compassion, or loving kindness to those on her team.

The complexities associated with such scenarios are endless. The point to remember is that each perspective is partial and true[97]— all depending on the complex interrelations between our human development stages, lines, and states and how those dimensions of self interface with our current life circumstances. Even within this framework, we are never one person or one stage all the time. We move up and down this mountain called life. The important thing to remember is that you have the power to change, the capacity to do and be more, and the heart to love with greater purpose and depth. The challenge is for you to fully reflect on your experience of time and money in the context of the dimensions of self that we've discussed. From this awareness, you can practice stewardship and step into radical abundance in ways that will give you a meaningful and prosperous personal and professional life.

To help position you to recognize how love manifests itself in this process, let's explore the basic premise of love in greater detail.

Love: An Outcome of the Cycle of Freedom™

The process underscoring the Cycle of Freedom™ goes like this: we develop greater awareness of our own storylines of time and money. We adopt a practice of stewardship. Stewardship in turn produces generosity. Generosity produces gratitude. Gratitude produces more compassion, and compassion ultimately produces the ultimate outcome of greater love. It is the love that produces a sense of radical abundance. When we love from our highest self, we experience abundance of the highest order. We experience joy.

Love is critical to our sense of meaning and purpose, but is love really a feeling, or is it an emotion, an action, a decision, or an agreement? Or is it all of these? This is an important question that has been a subject of great study for centuries. Throughout history, great minds have tried to capture and make sense of what love really means. This fact alone should alert us to the importance of love in our lives. Thousands of books have been written about love, and psychologists' offices are overflowing with people struggling with love. In our pop culture, love is Valentine's Day cards and candy, sexual exploitation, fantasy, celebrity reality shows of romance and roses. Even as adults, we engage in high-school infatuations, and our love desires splinter and fragment into our love of cars, shoes, season tickets, boats, make-up, designer jeans, two-story houses, and 65-inch plasma flat screen televisions.

In our pursuit for more time and money, is it possible, then, that at the root of our longings lies a deeper quest for love? For many of us, the chase for time and money is about acquiring more because we believe it will allow us to *be* more. If I *have* more, I can receive more power, control, and approval. But, what if we have it backwards? It's the old *have, do, be* equation. We think that we if just *had* more time and money, we could *do* all the things we want in life, and then we'd *be* happy.

What we currently understand about stages and lines of human development suggest otherwise. Our ability to grow up into later stages and lines of development, to include our cognitive, interpersonal, spiritual, moral, somatic, and emotional lines, supports our capacity for healthier perspectives. In willfully engaging in developmental growth, we increase our capacity to access our resources of time and money in healthier ways such that we shift the equation. We can *be* love such that we *do* life more fully: We live from a perspective of stewardship. We are generous with our time and money. We experience gratitude and compassion, and as a result, we *have* a more meaningful and prosperous life, irrespective of how much time or money is actually available to us. And, the good news is that this cycle is self-perpetuating. It goes on and on and on. The more we live in the Cycle of Freedom™, the more love we experience.

So, what's love got to do with it? Everything. "For where your treasure is, there your heart will be also."⁹⁸ Time and money are the treasure. What you do with this treasure points to that which you love most. How is your time and money being used to express or denigrate that love?

Throughout the course of humanity, we have searched for love. Love is the essence of who we are. So, it is with the other virtues of the Cycle of Freedom™. We are designed for goodness, and love is the core of this goodness. When it's absent from our life, for whatever reason, we are less than whole. When we are less than whole, we are no longer the gateway to love. We try to quickly, and sometimes irresponsibly, fill that emptiness. We squander our time or money on the very things that catapult us into a deeper chasm of emptiness only to wake one dark morning, eyes wide-open, and discover that we've only fallen deeper into an abyss of loneliness and despair. All our meaningless attempts to fill the hole with frivolous things, fruitless people, and dark places now prove futile.

But, here's more good news. Choosing to live in the Cycle of Freedom™ can help us realign our lives. That choice can open ourselves up as a gateway to generosity, gratitude, compassion, and the ultimate freedom of love. We can choose to *be* and *have* love.

Ultimately, love is the seat of the soul. Earlier, I spoke about the integration of the mind, body, and spirit. I stated the importance of this integration. The magical thread that holds this integration in place is love. Imagine that thread woven in and throughout your mind, your body, and your spirit. How differently might you think? How differently might you cherish your body? How much more alive and free would you feel? And when this magical thread of love is tightly woven and secured within, how much deeper and richer might your relationships be? How might you care for and serve the greater good of humanity?

Love: A Universal Language
Love solidifies our interpersonal connections and relationships. We are created from love and made to love, and this is why for generation upon generation, the great minds of theology, philosophy, and more recently, psychology have engaged in the quest for love on our behalf. What and how we love defines who we are. Egocentric choices or transgressions against this ultimate design for love destroy and splinter our soul.

A brief look into the theological, philosophical, and psychological perspectives on love reveals that love is, indeed, far more than a passing feeling. It is a universal language. It is how we intimately experience one another at a deep and profound level. As you will see from the brief discussion below, love is unique in that it the only earthly experience that supports each of us in realizing a more meaningful and prosperous life.

Theology and Love

For the purposes of understanding how love can help you realign your story toward radical abundance and a more meaningful and prosperous life, it is helpful to briefly look into different theological perspectives on love. Obviously, religious texts are voluminous and subject to constant interpretation, however for the purposes of helping you achieve meaning and purpose within the context of love and radical abundance, I will highlight one or two points from each of the five main religious texts.

I begin this discussion with theology because theology represents man's first search for meaning. Theology, in this context, relates to the systematic and rational study of concepts of God and of the nature of religious ideas in history and around the world. The words "systematic" and "rational" are particularly important, especially in this context, because they emphasize the scientific methodologies that seek to understand the nature of God, rather than the notion of God as an abstract concept somewhere in the stratosphere.

Hermeneutics, for example, is one such scientific methodology that addresses the study or interpretation of literary texts, more specifically the Bible, in an effort to gain deeper insight into the nature of God. Although it is less obvious in our modern culture, the connection between God and love as expressed across the five major world religions, namely, the Islamic, Jewish, Hinduism, Christian, and Buddhist traditions, have greatly influenced our societal perceptions on love. Regardless of the fundamental differences that exist between these religious traditions, each serves as evidence of our innate search for enlightenment and our need to know God and how God relates to love across the multiple dimensions of culture and religious tradition.

In the ancient Islamic tradition, for example, the *Qur'an*, viewed as a divine text, speaks to the one and only God or Allaah as great, merciful, kind, and just.[99] While the *Qur'an* does not specifically identify God *as* love, the concept of love is described at least 69 times in the *surahs* or chapters of the ancient text. These references to love, broken down into five categories include man's love of things, human love, man's love for God, God's love for man, and reasons why God withholds his love from those who transgress against the laws of the *Qur'an*. Such transgressions pertain to those who succumb to corruption and immorality, and include the wasting of resources or the boasting of riches.[100]

Even this brief synopsis of this very complex text suggests that the Islamic tradition points to the value and importance of love, and even stewardship, in all contexts of life.

In Judaism, the Hebrew words for love are *ahavah* and *chesed*, which can be translated as the intimate love of relationships and loving acts of kindness that include affection and compassion. According to 20th-century Jewish philosopher Franz Rosenzweig, the Torah communicates God's love for his people and how he demands their love in return. The sacred covenant of love between God and the Israelites was fulfilled when he brought them out of the slavery of Egypt and led them to the Promised Land.

Based on the Hebraic law of the Ten Commandments, the Israelites are called to love God above all else and to love their neighbors as they love themselves.

Editors Galli and Wolfson[101] add clarity to Rosenzweig's renowned work *The Star of Redemption,* by emphasizing his premise that "it is only love—God's love for us, the soul's love of God, and the orienting love of the neighbor, that endows life with a meaning that even death cannot erase."[102]

Each of the ancient religious texts is varied and uniquely complex with none perhaps subject to more interpretation than the Vedic texts of Hinduism which, among other things, emphasize liberation from rebirth to a preferred union with the divine as the ultimate goal.[103] In keeping with our theme of stewardship, one aspect of proper conduct is to avoid doing harm to any living being. In order to avoid conscious or deliberate violence against any living organism, to include the air we breathe or the water we drink, one must respect the divine in all things; hence, the belief in multiple gods. Additionally, the afterlife narratives as expressed in the *Upanishads* speak to the various fates that one might encounter upon death. For example, "those who are attached to earthly possessions, concerns, and desires travel with the effects of their earthly behavior 'to that very place to which his mind and character cling' before being reborn."[104]

In other words, one's fate in the afterlife is determined by moral, religious, or spiritual merit, or as expressed in a later version of the *Upanishads,* wisdom and knowledge. We might equate this belief to our discussion on the cognitive, spiritual, and moral lines of development. The varied expressions of the afterlife journey narratives as expressed in the *Rig Veda* speak to a concept of *moksha* that refers to liberation from a cycle of rebirth. According to the afterlife narratives, upon death, one can achieve immortality and remain in the afterlife with the universal deity, or one will be required to return to body and earth to repeat the cycle of life (reincarnation). The disciplines or practices associated with Hinduism, in their many forms, are, therefore, intended to offset worldly interests and selfish desires such that one achieves *moksha* or freedom.

To achieve *moksha*, one must overcome the six enemies of passion, hatred, greed, delusion, pride, and envy. Even if one is able to master these six enemies, the Vedas speak to an additional eight forms of pride that stand in the way of spiritual progress. These eight are particularly relevant to our discussion on time and money. They are pride of wealth, of physical strength, pride of youth, beauty, pride of knowledge, power, and even our penance. Pride is the source of many of these transgressions, so the work begins with examining the potential for thoughts, behaviors, and emotions associated with pride.

In the context of love, then, it might be said that the Hindu way of life requires that one values and respects every element of life here on earth even as one detaches from the "ways of the world" and seeks unity with the divine. From a Hindu perspective, then, *moksha* points to a recognized need to exactly what I've been suggesting all along: We are wise to stop the unhealthy chase for time and money. We are wiser still to pursue our own development such that we engage in the practice of stewardship so as to realize the outcomes of The Cycle of Freedom™.

Christianity, formulated a little over 2,000 years ago, is one of the more recent world religions. It expands upon the Hebraic understanding of God's love to include the sacrificial love of Jesus Christ. As the son or person of God, the death on the cross and resurrection of Jesus represent salvation and the ultimate love of God for all mankind. Christians are called to love as Jesus loved:

> Let us love one another, for love comes from God. Everyone who loves has been born of God and knows God. Whoever does not love does not know God, because God is love.[105]
>
> There is no fear in love. But perfect love drives out fear, because fear has to do with punishment. The one who fears is not made perfect in love. We love because he first loved us.[106]

Followers of Jesus, then, believe in a God of abundance, one who doesn't want them to live in fear or scarcity, a God who will provide. This belief, however, is often put to the test by the Biblical requirement of a 10% tithe of earnings to the church. For example, Christians who fall within the Expert or Achiever stage, may find it more challenging to expend their time, money, and talent on elements of the faith that emphasis time as eternal and tithes as a way to build the Kingdom of God.

Unbeknownst to many Christians, this "tithing" of time, money, and talent is more about how to build trusting relationship with a loving God that will provide than it is about supporting the needs of the church. Christians who might score in the High Abundance Time and Money categories or in the later stages of development might find this premise more palatable than those who measure at the High-to-Moderate Scarcity categories or even within the earlier stages. For those who do understand this premise of tithing time, money, and talent, however, such acts of generosity are viewed as an expression of Jesus' command to love God first and foremost and to love your neighbor as yourself.

The paradox of Christian love lies within this struggle between scarcity and the belief in a God of abundance and love. One of the primary distinctions between Islamic, Hebraic, and the Christian perspective on love has to do with the concept of grace. Grace, as defined in Christian theology, speaks to God's forgiveness of sins and what is referred to as unmerited favor. As sinners, Christians believe that they cannot earn salvation through their own merits. No amount of tithing or charitable good works will help them "buy" their way into the afterlife of Heaven. It is only through the infinite love and mercy of God and the power and grace of the Holy Spirit that one achieves redemption from sin and achieves life everlasting.[107] Since it is within our human nature to repeatedly sin against God and one another, and thereby, break the demands of love, Christians call upon the grace, power, and revelation of the Holy Trinity,[108] by way of Scripture and prayer, to strengthen and empower them to live out the daily demands of love in the midst of life's many challenging temptations—to include the many temptations associated with our quest for more time and money.

Finally, Buddhism, as one of the world's oldest universal religions, speaks to love within the underlying teachings of the Four Noble Truths.[109] While the many sects of Buddhism do not point to any central hierarchy, doctrine, or deity[110] as a focal point for worship or love, the ultimate goal of personal awakening and detachment allows for liberation from any of the typical trappings of love, e.g., falling in love (deemed as love out of our control) or lust.

The ancient teachings reveal that love, in its truest sense, is liberated from unhealthy attachment to desires or longings that may produce suffering. For many, Buddhism is believed to be a religion of love in that practices within most sects are intended to encourage personal enlightenment and nourish spiritual freedom. The four kinds of love encouraged in classical Buddhist teachings include: loving kindness, compassion, appreciative joy, and equanimity. Practices associated with the Eightfold Path are a means to end suffering through ethical behavior, meditation, and transcendent wisdom.[111]

The five major theological perspectives, in all their diverse complexity, indicate that humanity, throughout the ages, has sought deeper meaning and understanding of self and/or God, and that at the very core of our desire for understanding and enlightenment, in whatever form, is our quest for love.[112]

Next, came the analytical need to fit that which is unknowable into more rational thought. Enter the philosophical discourse of the ancient Greeks.

Philosophy and the Nature of Love

Philosophy seeks to understand the nature of love. Love and philosophy are deeply intertwined. Scholar and author Secomb states that Plato's *Symposium* offers "the most enduring and influential philosophical reflections on love"[113] because it explores the interrelationship between the earlier stage of erotic love and the passions of the mind to seek greater knowledge and truth.

Philosophy, known as "the love of wisdom," is more than logical analysis and a quest for reasoned argument.[114] It arises out of passion and a yearning for knowledge and understanding. The underlying premise of philosophy supports the premise that we are wired for passion, meaning, purpose, and ultimately—love.

Based on this philosophical perspective, love is "a constant process of becoming that involves searching for more."[115] Both philosophy and love are an ongoing search for good, beauty, and wisdom because "the attainment of these brings happiness."[116]

Plato's discussion on love is consistent with some aspects of the stages of development discussed in earlier chapters in that he contends that love is experienced in accordance with a developmental progression. In basic terms, Plato suggests that, in love, we are ultimately seeking beauty and goodness. Our life, then, is a perpetual search for things that will satisfy and fulfill our desire for beauty, goodness, and ultimately, happiness.[117]

Plato further contends that most are unaware of this perpetual search. I am further contending that this lack of awareness is what catapults us into scarcity and that how we attempt to fill this gap in our lives, this quest for love, is often demonstrated by our utilization of time and money. As we grow into a deeper perspective on love, we will come to adopt abundant perspectives on time and money. We will come to love in more meaningful and purposeful ways.

For purposes of our discussion on the stages and the various dimensions of self in relation to our experience of time and money, we might consider how the Strategist, for example, might more readily experience the type of love expressed by Plato than would those of us who engage in the incessant chase for more. Such distractions are a constant threat to our potential for love. Unless we commit to radical abundance by way of radical change, we may never reach Plato's fully expressed form of love.

The Psychology of Love

Until recent years, most psychological constructs focused more on the pathology of love than the elusive nature of love. By this I mean exploration into thoughts, emotions, and perceptions that indicate behaviors associated with the opposite of love: narcissism, pathological generosity, sexual perversion, abuse, alcoholism, and such similar acts of self-destructive behavior.

In recent years, psychologists have begun to explore scientific methodologies that are linked to theological and philosophical perceptions of love. This level of scientific investigation alerts us to the fact that even scientists now recognize our core and basic need for love; scientific methods are now being sought out as a way to determine and measure love as a solution to many of society's most damaging pathologies. Perhaps if we come to understand the nature of love in more scientific ways, we can begin to heal the disintegration among many who suffer from such disorders.

So it seems that since the beginning of time, it has been our essential nature to seek love. With theology, we seek enlightenment and attempt to know God as the ultimate source of love. With philosophy, we seek to know the nature of love itself, whereas in psychology, we seek our capacity for love of self and others. When we allow ourselves to chase time and money in unhealthy ways, we risk our capacity for love. We lose our potential for radical abundance in our lives.

A brief exploration into the theological and philosophical underpinnings of love, combined with what we know from a psychological and human developmental perspective, indicates that throughout history and around the world, mankind has sought a meaningful experience of life through his capacity to love. We are souls designed for love, and when we love, we are healed and transformed.

An Argument for Love

Many questions abound in the context of love whether from the perspective of theology or philosophy or the many modern-day psychological perspectives on love. Perhaps John Lennon had it right all along: All we need is love. Time and money, as windows into the soul, can serve as tangible and unique opportunities for us to explore our hearts and minds in relation to what and how we love.

It is not my intention to offer you a full and complete treatise on the virtues of the Cycle of Freedom™. Rather, my hope and desire is to whet your appetite for more love. When you shift your pursuit of time and money from a chase mentality of scarcity and fear to one that embodies acts of stewardship, generosity, gratitude, and compassion, you will experience freedom. And, from that freedom emerges love and a more meaningful, prosperous experience of life. This is not an easy process. Such a journey requires discipline, patience, and perseverance. What I can promise you is that it's worth the effort. What I can promise you is radical abundance such that you experience joy.

A Meaningful Life

We started this work together exploring your early-childhood stories and how they may have impacted your present-day experience of time and money. Your ability to embrace a meaningful life depends on your willingness to explore those stories, to examine them in relation to your existing thought patterns of either scarcity or abundance, and to perhaps engage in some purposeful changes. Embracing the practice of stewardship and the resultant outcomes of the Cycle of Freedom™ is one way to embrace those changes.

Holocaust survivor, neurologist, and psychiatrist Viktor Frankl reminds us that we have the power to choose our thoughts in the most dire of circumstances.[118] He also reminds us that the meaning of life is different for each and every one of us. We have a vocation or purpose or meaning that is often dependent on the circumstances of our life in any given moment. There is a time for survival, and there is a time for generosity, gratitude, compassion, and always for love.

It is in times of survival that we are called to live out our capacity for these virtues at the very highest order. It is in times of crisis that we, and those around us, need to more fully embody acts of stewardship and the Cycle of Freedom™. To be able to do so is the essence of radical abundance; it is the essence of love. Our capacity for a meaningful and prosperous life depends on our capacity for love. No matter what your current circumstances, this is your formula for living out your highest potential and your biggest life.

Frankl augments this belief by eloquently stating:

Ultimately, man should not ask what the meaning of his life is, but rather he must recognize that it is *he* who is asked. In a word, each man is questioned by life; and he can only answer to life by *answering for* his own life; to life he can only respond by being responsible.[119]

Part of our responsibility lies in how we think about life, how we make choices, and how we utilize our resources of time and money. I invite you to reflect on the childhood stories that may plague you still. Look not only to your childhood stories regarding time and money. Look to what they may have told you about yourself in relation to love. How have those stories enhanced your capacity for love? How have they held you captive to poverty mindsets of unworthiness, under-appreciation, greed, victimization, blame, or even cruelty? What needs to change in order for you to experience and express more love in your life? The difference between living a fractured life that constitutes a chase for more time and money and having a meaningful, prosperous life lies in your knowing the answers to these most difficult questions.

Remember, our mantra: *From the first moment of awareness comes opportunity for change.* You don't have to engage in an unhealthy chase for time and money. You can choose stewardship and the Cycle of Freedom™. And, you don't have to get it right the first time. All you have to do is engage in the habit of love such that you experience freedom in the daily moments called Life.

My hope and prayer is that you'll become the director of your own movie and that you'll choose radical abundance —and, in doing so, learn to love more fully!

Reflective Practice:

Chapter 15 focuses on the importance of love and how we can use our resources of time and money to demonstrate our love. This reflective practice is designed to help you consider time and money within the deeper context of love so that you can step into *radical abundance*. Radical abundance means that you practice stewardship such that you embody the traits of generosity, gratitude, and compassion. In doing so, you are now poised to pursue time and money in robust ways that support a meaningful, prosperous life.

Designate at least two hours to review the journal responses you have generated over the last few months. As you read through your entries, highlight any meaningful or jarring thoughts, emotions, or behaviors. Look for patterns that may have occurred and how those patterns reflect your capacity for either scarcity or abundance.

Reflect on those patterns and the actions you've taken with respect to those patterns. When you've completed this reflective time, spend at least 30 minutes responding to the following questions:

- What actions have you taken over the last several months in relation to those patterns?
- What changes do you still need to make in order to step more fully into radical abundance?
- In what ways can you use your resources to more fully demonstrate your love of others?

About the Author

Dr. Sharon Spano is a corporate business strategist, work force expert, and author of *Isabel's God*. Her work focuses on the empowerment of business leaders and entrepreneurs in an effort to help them maximize performance, improve employee engagement, and increase bottom-line results. As a Certified Professional Integral Coach™, Dr. Spano is dedicated to helping others adopt new paradigms about time and money so that they can step into radical abundance in every area of their lives. Her research focuses on wisdom, adult development, and leadership.

To learn more about possible speaking engagements, seminars, retreats, or integral coaching opportunities, please inquire at *www.SharonSpano.com*.

Appendix A

Appendix A

	HIGH MONEY SCARCITY	MODERATE MONEY SCARCITY	MODERATE MONEY ABUNDANCE	HIGH MONEY ABUNDANCE
	1.0-2.25	2.25-3.5	3.5-4.75	4.75-6.0
	"I will never have enough." Expressions of guilt, stress, helplessness, worry, or fear that may result in shame, anxiety, frustration, or anger about money.	"I must work hard to earn. I must be responsible." Expressions of worry, stress, or guilt if don't save. Fearful of spending money on "frivolous" things.	"I have the ability to earn the money I need for a better future." Expressions of satisfaction, happiness, balance, and fulfillment.	"I have the ability to create the money I need and share my resources with others." Expressions of peace, contentment, and joy
SELF-EFFICACY	**INADEQUATE** • Difficulty asking for compensation • Unable to place value on own time • May volunteer rather than earn to avoid accountability • Feels financially insecure	**MODERATE** • Works hard, but may not earn enough money • Money requires effort; Work may therefore seem burdensome • Belief that hard work, saving, and frugal spending will help meet basic needs • May not have sense of financial security beyond basic needs	**CAPABLE** • Ability to earn what is desired • Values money but is not controlled by it • Begins to understand the Flow of Money • Views money as exchange for goods and services • May have propensity for workaholism	**CREATIVE** • Identity is not based on how much money one has • Understands ability to create financial stability • Understands own financial story and how it impacts ability to create enough

Appendix A - continued

MONEY MATRIX

FINANCIAL RESPONSIBILITY

LACK OF FINANCIAL RESPONSIBILITY	FINANCIAL RESPONSIBILITY IS BURDENSOME	ASSUMES FINANCIAL RESPONSIBILITY	CREATES FINANCIAL RESPONSIBILITY
• No monthly/annual budget • No plan for earning, spending, saving • Consistent and ongoing debt/financial crisis • May feel like a victim to financial circumstances • Tendency to overspend or make poor financial choices • Views wealth/earning options for privileged few but not for self	• May be compulsive about money; unable to enjoy money • Hopes to teach children to be financially responsible; may cause them to be fearful instead • May avoid opportunities for calculated risks that could be profitable • May feel responsible for all financial outcomes without regard for contribution of other family members	• Good at balancing financial resources • Saves, spends, and invests wisely • Avoids unnecessary debt • Appreciates the need for financial security • May delay immediate self-gratification for longterm purchases, e.g.,home or car. • May use money as source of power.	• Is steward of resources in effort to contribute to greater needs of community and society-at-large • Sees responsibility as opportunity to effect social change • Earns, spends, saves, invests wisely • Understands flow of money and has ability to generate financial wealth

Appendix A - continued

	HIGH MONEY SCARCITY	MODERATE MONEY SCARCITY	MODERATE MONEY ABUNDANCE	HIGH MONEY ABUNDANCE
	1.0-2.25	2.25-3.5	3.5-4.75	4.75-6.0
ABILITY TO PLAN FOR FUTURE	**INABILITY TO THINK ABOUT FUTURE NEEDS:** • Operates from survival mentality that inhibits ability to visualize future needs • No will, trusts, retirement funds, savings, long-term investments. • Ignores future needs because does not believe in own ability to change financial situation.	**FOCUS IS ON IMMEDIATE FINANCIAL NEEDS:** • May manage money week-to-week or month-to-month but may not have wills, trusts, retirement funds, savings, or longer-term investments in place • May lack ability to fully enjoy life due to worry about running short of financial resources	**PLANS FOR FUTURE NEEDS:** • Accesses professional counsel to ensure that all resources are protected • Balanced perspective on work and play • Plans and saves for future needs, e.g., retirement.	**PLAN FOR FUTURE NEEDS IS BALANCED WITH DESIRED LIFESTYLE:** • Works and plays hard • Allows for luxury items of enjoyment, e.g., gifts, vacations, home, cars. • Lives within means

Appendix A - continued

MONEY MATRIX

POTENTIAL FOR GENEROSITY

LACK OF GENEROSITY	FORCED GENEROSITY	SELECTIVE GENEROSITY	GENEROUS HEART
• Inability to give to others for fear of not having enough for basic needs • May engage in bouts of egocentric spending that hinders ability to share or contribute to others	• Gives out of obligation rather than from generous heart • Fearful of running out of resources and not being able to fulfill financial obligations to own family	• Contributes as long as giving doesn't interfere with own lifestyle • Contributes because it is the "right thing to do" in eyes of others	• Contributes from spirit of generosity • Focus is on serving greater good of humanity • Sees money as blessing

Appendix B

	HIGH MONEY SCARCITY	MODERATE TIME SCARCITY	MODERATE TIME ABUNDANCE	HIGH TIME ABUNDANCE
	1.0–2.25	2.25–3.5	3.5–4.75	4.75–6.0
	"I never have enough time to get it all done."	*"I must be productive and exercise efficient use of time"*	*"Time is fleeting. I should manage it well."*	*"Time is a precious resource. I should enjoy every moment."*
EXPRESSIONS:	• Feelings of constraint or overwhelm • Frustration • Sense of being chased • Feelings of guilt if not productive • May feel as though they have no control over day	• Torn between time with family and work • May have feelings of guilt, anxiousness, stress, frustration when not being productive • Sense of being constrained by time	• Sense of focus • Appreciates flexibility • Sense of control over own time • May enjoy sense of balance • Enjoys and appreciates rest and relaxation	• Sense of control over own life; freedom to choose how time is utilized • Fully present in daily moments of life • Gratitude and joy • Free from guilt when relaxing or taking time with loved ones

Appendix B - continued

TIME MATRIX

	INADEQUATE	MODERATE	CAPABLE	PROACTIVE
SELF-EFFICACY	• May lack ability to plan or focus	• Workaholic potential	• Believes in balance between work and family	• Manages time as if finest treasure
	• May lose track of time	• May have over stringent time management practices	• Sets realistic expectations	• Great at prioritizing daily activities/events
	• Busy but not effective	• Slave to schedule or calendar	• Uses time with discretion	• Works and plays equally well
	• May procrastinate	• Honors commitments	• Present in moment	• Reliable and consistent behaviors related to time
	• May be crisis driven and addicted to urgency	• Believes it important to be early or on time to appointments	• Prioritizes time well	• May enjoy time alone for contemplation
	• May not experience meaningful outcomes	• Must keep busy and productive	• May be good at multitasking	• Values other people's time
	• May be overly cautious about use of time due to early childhood induced fear of wasting it	• Good at multi-tasking	• Often considerate of other's time	
	• May shut down when overwhelmed	• Tries to use time wisely	• May be overly confident about ability to manage and take on too much	

Appendix B - continued

EXPERIENCE OF TIME	HIGH MONEY SCARCITY 1.0-2.25	MODERATE TIME SCARCITY 2.25-3.5	MODERATE TIME ABUNDANCE 3.5-4.75	HIGH TIME ABUNDANCE 4.75-6.0
	• Passes too quickly • Everything is priority • Time is stressful • Not enough time in day • Everything must be done now!	• Time is scarce • Time is money • Time is fleeting; finite • Time goes faster with age • Time is a limited commodity	• Time is neutral/finite commodity • Must be managed • Time is a continuum that marks the passing of events • Time is always there, a constant • Time is fleeting; don't waste it; make self useful • Time is relative • Time quickens with age	• Time is precious/use wisely • Time is both abstract and concrete • Time should be balanced between work and family • Free time is important; don't waste time on things you don't enjoy • Make the most of every moment • Time is the most valuable thing in life • Time is as valuable as money

TIME MATRIX

Appendix B - continued

			GENEROUS HEART
SENSE OF ACCOMPLISHMENT	Non-existent no matter how much actually gets done	Works very hard all day, may accomplish goals but feels as though accomplishes little	• Sense of accomplishment that is not necessarily linked to how much was actually done • Belief that anything can be accomplished • Produces results	• "Live with no regrets" attitude • Balanced perspective on life • Intentional about what is to be accomplished
	LACK OF GENEROSITY	**SPORADIC GENEROSITY**	**INTENTIONAL GENEROSITY**	**GENEROUS HEART**
POTENTIAL FOR GENEROSITY	• May disregard other people's time • Procrastination may create undue stress on others	• Giving of one's time is valued in relation to honoring time commitments and being on time • Time for family/recreation may be more task oriented than relational • Efficient use of time includes perspectives on being productive, helping others, and rest and relaxation; may not do this consistently	• Values moments with loved ones • Desires time for others but may struggle with how to balance with work commitments • Always on time/conscious of others' time	• Freely gives time to family and those in need without expressed feelings of guilt or shame • Enjoys the moment • Time with loved ones is memory-making

STAGES OVERVIEW IN RELATION TO TIME AND MONEY

Meta Aware	**Illumined 6.5**	Perspective includes an integrated whole that sees time in terms of eternity and infinity. Prioritization and categorization no longer a struggle; experiences nested worlds of matter, life, and mind.
	Universal 6.0	Kosmos-centric, 6th person perspective; experience of divine and mystical; goes beyond and includes all human concrete groups and subtle systems. Priorities don't arise easily as all things are interconnected; lives in moment.
	Transpersonal 5.5	Can prioritize endless elements of interest; time and money may be utilized to solve human suffering; has a cosmic planetary space frame.
	Construct Aware 5.0	Historical time frame; sees multiple generations and multiple perspectives. Experiences time and space in fundamentally different way via witnessing awareness. Broader space to hold love. Can let go of story.
Subtle Tier	**Strategist 4.5**	Multi-generational time scheme. See minimum of 25+ years out in terms of own lifetime and past and future generations; prioritizes competing commitments, beliefs, and opinions. Planet-centric: May utilize time and money to impact broader integrated systems, e.g. support of ecosystems.
	Pluralist 4.0	Sees parent/child in lifetime. Sees 10+ years backward and forward but is present focused. Relationships and process valued over goals so may lose track of time and frustrate others as result.
	Achiever 3.5	Sees 5 years into future; tendency to chase time and money; focused on goal orientation. Ethnocentric viewpoint; competitive with others. May struggle with balancing work, family, and play and use of time/money accordingly.
	Expert 3.0	Sees past and present and 2-3 years into future. Cannot prioritize or categorize well. Limited time/money capacity; may lose track of time and go over budget. Focus on efficiency over effectiveness; may miss deadlines or waste money due to perfectionistic or micromanagement tendencies.
Concrete Tier	**Conformist 2.5**	Sees today and past but can't project into future. Can prioritize and conform to rules of the group, so may utilize time and money based on norms of immediate group. Can delay gratification and anticipate consequences. Views money as reward or symbol of group acceptance.
	Rule-Oriented 2.0	Beginning to learn from past mistakes. Main focus is immediate needs so may utilize time and money in impulsive ways; cannot prioritize well so may fail to plan for future.
	Opportunist 1.5	Can include people up to age 5. Learning to visualize; Egocentric viewpoint; everything is mine; no sense of fairness or reciprocity. Can't learn from past mistakes.
	Impulsive 1.0	Babies and children, 6-18 months. No visualization; kinesthetic memory only. Focus on getting concrete needs met.

Adapted from the StAGES Model of O'Fallon, 2016

DEFINITIONS OF PRIMARY LINES
OF HUMAN DEVELOPMENT

Developmental lines are complex and varied. Leading theorists contend that we have at least twenty-six lines of development that support us in who we are. The following primary six lines of development are further explicated based on the work of Divine & Hunt in an effort to help the reader discern areas that may warrant further consideration for future adult development. Each is relevant to our experience of time and money and life in general.

Cognitive	Awearness of What Is	The capacity to see from different perspectives, the value, synergies, and implications of those perspectives, and to do so through space and time.
Emotional	The Spectrum of Emotions	The capacity to access, include and skillfully be present to and interacting in the emotional field of self and others.
Somatic	Body/Mind Awareness	The capacity to access, include and skillfully draw upon the energies of the gross, subtle, and causal realms.
Interpersonal	How I Socially Relate to Others	The capacity to relate to and communicate with others in a way that all perspectives (I, Thou, We, It) are attended to at the appropriate level.
Spiritual	The Ultimate Concern	The capacity to explore the ultimate concern. "Who Am I? Why Am I Here? What am I to do? Where do I go from here?)
Moral	Awareness of What to Do?	The capacity to reach a moral decision involving both moral judgment and care; attend to the moral span it encompasses (from me to us to all of us to all sentient beings).

Written with permission from Divine & Hunt, Integral Coaching Canada.

Bibliography

Akhtar, Salman. "Normal and Pathological Generosity." *Psychoanalytic Review* 99, no. 5 (2012): 646–62.

Amir, Lydia. "Plato's Theory of Love: Rationality as Passion." *The British Journal of Philosophical Practice* 4, no. 3 (2001): 6-14. http://www.society-for-philosophy-in-practice.org/journal/pdf/4-3%2006%20Amir%20-%20Plato%20Love.pdf.

Argyle, Michael, and Adrian Furnham. *The Psychology of Money.* London: Routledge, 2008.

Bandura, Albert. *Self-Efficacy: The Exercise of Control.* New York: W.H. Freeman and Company, 1997.

Block, Peter. *Stewardship: Choosing Service Over Self-Interest.* San Francisco: Berrett-Koehler Publishers, 2013.

Brown, Barrett Chapman. "Conscious Leaders for Sustainability: How Leaders with a Late-Stage Action Logic Design and Engage in Sustainability Initiatives." PhD diss., Fielding Graduate University, 2012.

Buck, Ross. "The Gratitude of Exchange and the Gratitude of Caring." In *The Psychology of Gratitude,* eds. Robert A. Emmons and Michael E. McCullough, 100. New York: Oxford University Press, 2004.

Capra, Fritjof. *The Web of Life: A New Scientific Understanding of Living Systems.* New York: Anchor Books, 1996.

Coleman, James William. *The New Buddhism.* New York: Oxford University Press, 2001. Accessed April 11, 2016. http://www.ahandfulofleaves.org/documents/The%20New%20Buddhism%20The%20Western%20Transformation%20of%20an%20Ancient%20Tradition_Coleman.pdf.

Cook-Greuter, Susanne. *"Ego Development: Nine Levels of Increasing Embrace."* Unpublished manuscript, 2005. http://www.slideshare.net/UnitB166ER/ego-development-nine-levels-of-increasing-embrace-susanne-r-cookgreuter-ed-d-codirector-of-the-ii-psychology-center.

—. "Mature Ego Development." Adapted and revised from *Journal of Adult Development* 7, no. 4 (2000): 227-40.

Covey, Stephen R., and A. Roger Merrill. *First Things First.* London: Simon & Schuster, 1994.

Dayton, Howard L. *Your Money Counts: The Biblical Guide to Earning, Spending, Saving,Investing, Giving, and Getting Out of Debt.* Orlando: Compass-Finances God's Way, 2011.

Diprose, Rosalyn. *Corporeal Generosity: On Giving with Nietzsche, Merleau-Ponty, and Levinas.* Albany: State University of New York Press, 2002.

Divine, Laura, and Joanne Hunt, eds. *ICCP-1 Associate Certification Module.* Ottawa: Integral Coaching Canada, Inc., 20130.

Elby, Tristan. "A Contemporary Guide to the Vedas: A Critical Survey of the Tests and Literature." *Religion Compass* 8 (2014): 128–38.

Elias, Mufti Afzal Hoosen. *Qur'aan Made Easy.* Lenasia: EDI Publishers, 2011.

Emmons, Robert A., and Michael E. McCullough, eds. *The Psychology of Gratitude.* New York: Oxford University Press, 2004.

Esbjorn-Hargens, Sean. "An Overview of Integral Theory: An All-Inclusive Framework for the 21st Century." *Integral Institute* 1 (2009): 1–24.

Firth, Paul, Hui Zheng, Jeremy S. Windsor, Andrew I. Sutherland, Christopher H. Imray, G.W.K. Moore, John L. Semple, Robert C. Roach and Richard A. Salisbury. "Mortality on Mount Everest, 1921–2006: Descriptive Study," *BMJ: British Medical Journal* 337, no. 7684:a2654 (2008), doi: 10.1136/bmj.a2654.

Frankl, Viktor. *Man's Search for Meaning.* New York: Simon & Schuster, 1984.

Fredrickson, Barbara L. "Gratitude, Like Other Positive Emotions, Broadens and Builds." In *The Psychology of Gratitude,* eds. Robert A. Emmons and Michael E. McCullough, 145. New York: Oxford University Press, 2004.

Fronsdal, Gil. "The Buddha's Teaching on Love." *Insight Meditation Center.* Accessed April 11, 2016. http://www.insightmeditationcenter.org/books-articles/articles/the-buddhas-teachings-on-love/

Furnham, Adian, Kate Telford and Emma Wilson. "The Meaning of Money: The Validation of a Short Money-Types Measure." *Personality and Individual Differences* 52, no. 6 (2012): 707-11.

Gillman, Peter. ed. *Everest-The Best Writing and Pictures from Seventy Years of Human Endeavor.* New York: Little, Brown and Company, 1993.

Greenberg, Mark T., and Christa Turksma. "Understanding and Watering the Seeds of Compassion." *Research in Human Development* 12, no. 3-4 (2015): 280-87.

Goldsmith, Marshall, and Mark Reiter. *Triggers: Creating Behavior Change That Lasts- Becoming the Person You Want to Be.* New York: Crown Publishing Group, 2015.

Hatch, Mary Jo, and Ann L. Cunliffe. *Organization Theory.* New York: Oxford University Press, 2006.

Heard, Matt. *Life with a Capital L: Embracing Your God-Given Humanity.* Colorado Springs: Multnomah Books, 2015.

Kegan, Robert. *The Evolving Self: Problem and Process in Human Development.* Cambridge: Harvard University Press, 1982.

Leopold, A. Carl. "Stewardship." In *Encyclopedia of Applied Ethics* 4, ed. Ruth F. Chadwick. (1998): 225-32.

Li-Ping Tang, Thomas. "Theory of Monetary Intelligence: Money Attitudes-Religious Values, Making Money, Making Ethical Decisions, and Making the Grade." *Journal of Business Ethics* 133, no. 3 (2016): 583-603.

Loevinger, Jane. *Ego Development.* San Francisco: Jossey-Bass, 1976.

Mahally, Farid. "A Study of the Word 'love' in the Qur'an." *Answering Islam.* Accessed April 2, 2016. *http://*www.answering-islam.org/ Quran/Themes/love.htm.

McCauley, Cynthia D. , Wilfred H. Drath, Charles J. Palus, Patricia M.G. O'Connor and Becca A. Baker. "The Use of Constructive-Developmental Theory to Advance the Understanding of Leadership." *The Leadership Quarterly* 17 (2006): 634–53.

McCuddy, Michael, and Wendy L. Pirie. "Spirituality, Stewardship, and Financial Decision-Making." *Managerial Finance* 33, no. 12 (2007): 957-69.

McKnight, John, and Peter Block. *The Abundant Community: Awakening the Power of Families and Neighborhoods.* San Francisco: Berrett-Kohler Publishers, 2010.

Mind and Life Education Research Network, "Contemplative Practices and Mental Training: Prospects for American Education." *Child Development Perspectives* 6, no. 2 (2012): 146-53.

Morgan, Gareth. *Images of Organization*. Thousand Oaks: Sage Publications, 2006.

Neff, Kristin D., Kristin L. Kirkpatrick and Stephanie S. Rude. "Self-Compassion and Adaptive Psychological Functioning." *Journal of Research in Personality* 41 (2007): 139-54.

O'Fallon, Terri. *StAGES: Growing up is Waking Up – Interpenetrating Quadrants, States and Structures*. Unpublished manuscript (May, 2016).

Orthberg, John. *Soul Keeping: Caring for the Most Important Part of You*. Grand Rapids: Zondervan, 2014.

Parish, Ria. "Content is King – Bill Gates, 1996." Online Marketing *(blog). Silkstream* http://www.silkstream.net/blog/2014/07/content-is-king-bill-gates-1996.html.

Rosenthal, Seth, and Todd L. Pittinsky. "Narcissistic Leadership." *Leadership Quarterly* 17, no. 6 (2006): 617-33.

Rosenzweig, Franz. *The Star of Redemption,* eds. Barbara E. Galli and Elliot R. Wolfson. Madison: The University of Wisconsin Press, 2005.

Spano, Sharon. "Complexity Theory: A New Paradigm for Leadership." Unpublished manuscript 2010: 1-25.

Secomb, Linnell. *Philosophy and Love: From Plato to Popular Culture*. Edinburgh: Edinburgh University Press, 2007.

Shelton, Charles M. *The Gratitude Factor: Enhancing Your Life through Grateful Living*. Mahwah: Paulist Press, 2010.

Shushan, Gregory. "Afterlife Conceptions in the Vedas." *Religion Compass* 5, no. 6 (2011): 202-13.

Sproul, Kathleen, ed. *The Shorter Bartlett's Familiar Quotations*. New York: Pocket Books, 1965.

Stacey, Ralph. "The Science of Complexity: An Alternative Perspective for Strategic Change Processes." *Strategic Management Journal* 16, no.6 (1995): 477-95. DOI 10.1002/smj.4250160606

The Tudors. Created by Michael Hirst. Toronto, Ontario, Canada: Peace Arch Entertainment, 2007. http://www.sho.com/sho/the-tudors/home.

The Wolf of Wall Street. Directed by Martin Scorsese. 2013. Hollywood, CA: Paramount Pictures, 2013. DVD.

Torbert, William R. *Managing the Corporate Dream: Restructuring for Long-Term Success.* Homewood: Dow Jones-Irwin, 1987.

Torbert, William R., Susanne Cook-Greuter, Dalmar Fisher, Erica Foldy, Alain Gautheir, Jackie Keeley and David Rooke, et al. *Action Inquiry: The Secret of Timely and Transforming Leadership.* San Francisco: Berrett-Koehler Publishers, 2004.

Twist, Lynne. *The Soul of Money: Reclaiming the Wealth of Our Inner Resources.* New York: W.W. Norton & Company, 2003.

Welp, Laura R. and Christina M. Brown. "Self-Compassion, Empathy, and Helping Intentions." *The Journal of Positive Psychology* 9, no. 1 (2013): 54-65.

Wilber, Ken. *The Collected Works of Ken Wilber.* Boston: Shambhala Publishing, 1999-2000.

—. *Integral Psychology: Consciousness, Spirit, Psychology, Therapy.* Boston: Shambhala Publications, 2000.

—. *A Brief History of Everything.* Boston: Shambhala Publications, 2000.

—. *Integral Spirituality: A Startling New Role for Religion in the Modern and Postmodern World.* Boston: Shambhala Publications, 2006.

Zimbardo, Paul G., and John N. Boyd. *The Time Paradox: The New Psychology of Time That Will Change Your Life.* New York: Free Press, 2009.

Endnotes

Chapter 2

1   Marshall Goldsmith, *Triggers: Creating Behavior Change That Lasts; Becoming the Person You Want to Be.* (New York: Crown Publishing Group, 2015).

2   Susanne Cook-Greuter, *"Ego Development: Nine Levels of Increasing Embrace."* Unpublished manuscript (2005); Robert Kegan, *The Evolving Self: Problem and Process in Human Development* (Cambridge: Harvard University Press, 1982); Jane Loevinger, *Ego Development* (San Francisco: Jossey-Bass, 1976); William R. Torbert et al., *Action Inquiry: The Secret of Timely and Transforming Leadership* (San Francisco: Berrett-Koehler Publishers, 2004).

3   Ken Wilber, *Integral Psychology: Consciousness, Spirit, Psychology, Therapy* (Boston: Shambhala Publications, 2000); Ken Wilber,

Integral Spirituality: A Startling New Role for Religion in the Modern and Postmodern World (Boston: Shambhala Publications, 2006); Laura Divine and Joanne Hunt, eds., *ICCP-1 Associate Certification Module.* (Ottawa:Integral Coaching Canada, Inc., 2013).

4   Wilber, *Integral Spirituality.*

5   Ibid., 6.

6   Michael Argyle and Adrian Furnham, *The Psychology of Money.* (London: Routledge, 2008).

7   Adian Furnham et al., "The Meaning of Money: The Validation of a Short Money-Types Measure," *Personality and Individual Differences 52* (2012): 707-11.

Chapter 3

8   Gareth Morgan, *Images of Organization* (Thousand Oaks: Sage Publications, Inc., 2006); Mary Jo Hatch and Ann L. Cunliffe, *Organization Theory* (New York: Oxford University Press, 2006).

9   Morgan, *Images of Organization.*

10   Luke 12:34 (NIV)

Chapter 4

11   Lynne Twist. *The Soul of Money: Reclaiming the Wealth of Our Inner Resources* (New York: W.W. Norton & Company, 2003).

12   John Ortberg, *Soul Keeping: Caring for the Most Important Part of You* (Grand Rapids: Zondervan, 2014).

13   Ibid.

Chapter 5

14   Thomas Li-Ping Tang, "Theory of Monetary Intelligence: Money Attitudes-Religious Values, Making Money, Making Ethical

Decisions, and Making the Grade," *Journal of Business Ethics* 133, no. 3 (2016): 583-603.

15   Ibid.

16   Michael McCuddy and Wendy L. Pirie, "Spirituality, Stewardship, and Financial Decision-Making," *Managerial Finance* 33, no.12 (2007): 957-69.

17   To access the Time and Money Inventory that resulted in these initial themes, please go to: www.SharonSpano.com.

18   These Major Storylines are explicated and compared in relation to the Major Storylines associated with abundance in Appendix A.

19   *The Wolf of Wall Street*, Directed by Martin Scorsese. United States: Paramount, 2013.

20   Seth Rosenthal, and Todd L. Pittinsky, "Narcissistic Leadership," *Leadership Quarterly* 17.6 (2006): 617-33.

21   *The Tudors.* Canada: Peace Arch Entertainment, 2007. url: www.sho.com/the-tudors/home.

Chapter 6

22   John McKnight and Peter Block, *The Abundant Community: Awakening the Power of Families and Neighborhoods* (San Francisco: Berrett-Kohler Publishers, 2010).

23   Stephen R. Covey and A. Roger Merrill, *First Things First* (London: Simon & Schuster, 1994).

Chapter 8

24   Peter Gillman, ed. *Everest-The Best Writing and Pictures from Seventy Years of Human Endeavor.* (New York: Little, Brown and Company, 1993).

25 Paul Firth, "Mortality on Mount Everest, 1921–2006: Descriptive Study," *BMJ: British Medical Journal* 337, no. 7684:a2654 (2008), doi: 10.1136/bmj.a2654.

26 McCauley et al., "The Use of Constructive-Developmental Theory," 634–53.

27 Kegan, *The Evolving Self,* 1982; Cook-Greuter, "Mature Ego Development," 2000; Torbert, *Managing the Corporate Dream,*1987.

28 McCauley et al., "The Use of Constructive-Developmental Theory," 636.

29 Even though theorists do not consider the stages of development to be hierarchal in nature, the analogy of a mountain or ladder is sometimes used to offer a visual perspective on human development in that all stages arise and transcend and give even as we are still able to access the perspectives of earlier stages. Renowned theorists in the field, e.g., Cook-Greuter and Torbert have their own descriptors for the various stages. For purposes of my own work, I speak to the StAGES Model developed by researcher Terri O'Fallon. For more information on the StAGES assessment, please go to www.PacificIntegral.com.

30 Terri O'Fallon, personal communication, 2014.

31 Ken Wilber, *A Brief History of Everything* (Boston: Shambhala Publications, 2000).

32 Ibid., 132.

33 As a certified Integral Coach, I can attest to this methodology as one path to self-discovery. Another might be to take the StAGES Assessment offered at www.PacificIntegral.com.

34 Wilber, *A Brief History.*

35 Divine, *Integral Coaching Manual.*

36 Ibid.

37   Cook- Greuter, "Ego Development,"; Kegan, *The Evolving Self*,; Loevinger, *Ego Development*; Torbert et al., *Action Inquiry*.

38   Wilber, *A Brief History*.

39   Wilber, *Integral Spirituality*.

Chapter 9

40   Each of the major theorists in the field has a slightly different name of the twelve stages of human development as we currently understand them. For purposes of this body of work, I am utilizing the categorizations of Dr. Terri O'Fallon. According to her research, the stages are defined as: Impulsive, Opportunist, Rule-Oriented, Conformist, Expert, Achiever, Pluralist, Strategist, Meta-Aware, Transpersonal, Universal, and Illumined. Each stage is complex unto itself. I am only addressing the Conformist through Strategist stages because these stages represent the most relevant population in relation to this body of work. I am also limiting my comments to the dimensions of the stages that will be most useful to the reader's understanding of their time and money experience. For greater detail on the complex nuances of the stages, please visit www.PacificIntegral. com.

41   These distinctions reference the work of Terri O'Fallon. Other theorists often refer to these differentiations as Pre-Conventional, Conventional, and Post-Conventional. No matter how the tiers are expressed, they represent concrete and abstract variations in thinking.

42   Barrett Chapman Brown, "Conscious Leadership for Sustainability: How Leaders with a Late-Stage Action Logic Design and Engage in Sustainability Initiatives," (PhD dissertation, Fielding Graduate University, 2011).

43   These leaders were scored using the SCTI-Map of Suzanne Cook-Greuter.

44   Terri O'Fallon, "StAGES in Depth: Growing Up is Waking Up– Interpenetrating Quadrants, States and Structures," Unpublished manuscript (May, 2016).

45   Brown, "Conscious Leadership."

46   Ibid.

47   Ibid.

48   Ibid.

49   Ibid.

Chapter 10

50   There is a great amount of research in support of complexity and chaos theory. While there is no agreed upon theory with respect to complexity, researchers do share a common interest in certain properties to include patterns of self-organization and order within chaos, emergence, learning and adaptation, and distance of equilibrium in conjunction with dissipative structures. Overall, complexity theory stems from a conglomeration of theories and findings within a variety of disciplines that shift understanding of prior reductionist perspectives to greater emphasis on nonlinear dynamic systems that are constantly in the state of flux, to include processes of adaptation, learning, and evolution. (Sharon Spano, "Complexity Theory: A New Paradigm for Leadership," Unpublished manuscript (2010): 1–25; See: Fritjof Capra, *The Web of Life: A New Scientific Understanding of Living Systems* (New York: Anchor Books, 1996). Self-organization is defined as a process by which a system creates its own order and new forms of order emerge, which in turn allows for additional processes to evolve that ultimately create order from disorder (Ibid.,). Nonlinear

dynamic systems make it impossible for us to discuss properties in a linear fashion, but complexity theory examines the patterns of these dynamic mechanisms and how they adapt and emerge. In short, a sudden shift in the stock market as we witnessed in 2008 is an example of nonlinear emergence. This shift was not the result of actions on the part of one individual or one group. Simply stated, agents can choose whether or not to follow the rules, and, depending on the nature of that choice, generate stable or unstable environments. As individual citizens, the question then becomes, how much did our own personal sense of greed and irresponsibility contribute to the shift in the market? More importantly, what must we do as individuals to acknowledge and prepare for the reality that, from a systems approach, behaviors, economic or otherwise, are unpredictable over the long term? My point here is that each of us has the potential to recognize our own patterns of behavior with respect to time and money such that we contribute to patterns of self-organization and order within ever-evolving markets. Researcher Stacey reminds us, "Internal spontaneous organization amongst the agents of a system, when provoked by instabilities, can potentially lead to emergent order." See: Ralph Stacey, "The Science of Complexity: An Alternative Perspective for Strategic Change Processes," *Strategic Management Journal* 16, no.6 (1995): 477–95.

51 Matthew 6:21 (NIV)
52 Peter Block, *Stewardship: Choosing Service Over Self-Interest* (San Francisco: Berrett-Koehler Publishers, 2013).
53 Ibid.
54 Ibid.
55 Ibid.
56 McCuddy, "Spirituality, Stewardship," 957–69.

57   Ibid., 958.

58   Ibid.

59   Ibid., 960.

60   Ria Parish, "Content is King-Bill Gates, 1996," Online Marketing (blog), Silkstream, http://www.silkstream.net/blog/2014/07/content-is-king-bill-gates-1996.html. The phrase became a mantra for internet marketers as a result of a memo from Bill Gates to the Microsoft staff on May 26, 1995 entitled, "The Internet Tidal Wave," (accessed April 6, 2016). Today, many content marketers would add that while content is important, knowing how to market the content via the internet is equally important.

61   Howard L. Dayton, *Your Money Counts: The Biblical Guide to Earning, Spending, Saving, Investing, Giving, and Getting Out of Debt* (Orlando: Compass-Finances God's Way, 2011).

62   Block, *Stewardship.*

63   A. Carl Leopold, "Stewardship," in *Encyclopedia of Applied Ethics, 4* (San Diego: Academic Press, 1998).

64   McKnight, *The Abundant Community.*

65   Ibid.

66   McCuddy, "Spirituality, Stewardship."

Chapter 12

67   Paul G. Zimbardo and John N. Boyd, *The Time Paradox* (New York: Free Press, 2009).

68   Ibid.

69   Albert Bandura, *Self-Efficacy: The Exercise of Control* (New York: W.H. Freeman and Company, 1997).

Chapter 13

70   Integral Integral Theory offers a very complex framework that is crucial to our discussion on time and money. However, for purposes of this body of work, I am only utilizing the AQAL Model as a tool to help the reader develop awareness of their own internal conversations on time on money as depicted in Figure 1. "The Integral Model on Time, Money, and Stewardship" as depicted in Figure 1 is adapted from Wilber's AQAL Model and can be accessed for further exploration through any one of his collected works. First time explorers might begin with Wilber, A Brief History of Everything, 2000. The idea for the questions outlined in Figure 2 came from the work of Divine and Hunt at www.IntegralCoachingCanada, Inc. As a certified integral coach, I am honored to engage in this level of work with my clients and to be a part of the extended in-depth work of Divine and Hunt.

71   Sean Esbjorn-Hargens, "An Overview of Integral Theory: An All-Inclusive Framework for the 21st Century," *Integral Institute* 1 (2009): 1–24.

72   Ken Wilber, *The Collected Works of Ken Wilber*, (Boston: Shambhala Publishing, 1999-2000).

73   Esbjorn-Hargens, "An Overview of Integral Theory."

74   AQAL stands for "all-quadrants, all lines, and all levels" The model has been expanded to include other frameworks such as "all types," but the initial framework applied to discourse related to states, stages, and lines of human development as set forth in Wilber's earlier work.

75   Sean Esbjorn-Hargens is associate professor and founding chair of the Department of Integral Theory at John F. Kennedy University. He is a leading scholar-practitioner in integral theory

and founder and executive editor of the Journal of Integral Theory and Practice.

76 Esbjorn-Hargens, "An Overview of Integral Theory."

77 In the simplest form, Wilber explains the "interior" and "exterior" aspects of the AQAL Model to involve perception and interpretation respectively. The left-hand or interior aspects of the model speaks to what something means whereas the right-hand or exterior aspects of the model addresses what something does. For example, the upper-left quadrant corresponds to thoughts and emotions, aspects of self that cannot be seen but require interpretation where as the upper-right quadrant corresponds to behaviors, acts that can be seen. These aspects of the model are then included within the framework from a collective standpoint as well, e.g., the values of a culture in the lower-left vs. the external systems of the collective in the lower-right. See: Wilber, *A Brief History*, 82-83.

78 After thirty-plus years of research, several validated assessments have been developed and are available for those who may want to gather hard data on where they land in terms of stages, states, and lines of human development. For more information on these assessments go to: www.verticaldevelopment.com; www.williamtorbert.com/global-leadership-profile/; or www. pacificintegral.com. These sites represent the work of Cook-Greuter, Torbert, and O'Fallon respectively.

79 Visual representations of various renditions of the AQAL Model can be found in Wilber, *A Brief History*.

Chapter 14

80 Salman Akhtar, "Normal and Pathological Generosity," *Psychoanalytic Review* 99:5 (2012): 646–62.

81 Ibid.

82 Rosalyn Diprose, *Corporeal generosity: On Giving with Nietzsche, Merleau=Ponty, and Levinas* (Albany: State University of New York Press, 2002) 2.

83 Oxforddictionaries.com, s.v. "Gratitude," accessed March 2, 2016, http://www.oxforddictionaries.com/us/definition/american_english/gratitude.

84 Barbara L. Fredrickson, "Gratitude, Like Other Positive Emotions, Broadens and Builds," in *The Psychology of Gratitude*, ed. Robert A. Emmons and Michael E. McCullough (New York: Oxford University Press, 2004), 145.

85 Charles M. Shelton, *The Gratitude Factor: Enhancing Your Life through Grateful Living* (Mahwah: Hidden Spring, 2010).

86 Ibid.

87 Ibid.

88 Robert A. Emmons and Michael E. McCullough, eds., *The Psychology of Gratitude* (New York: Oxford University Press, 2004).

89 Ross Buck, "The Gratitude of Exchange and the Gratitude of Caring," in *The Psychology of Gratitude*, ed. Robert A. Emmons and Michael E. McCullough (New York: Oxford University Press, 2004), 100.

90 Ibid. Quote originally published in K. Sproul, ed., The Shorter Bartlett's Familiar Quotations (New York: Pocket Books, 1965) 314.

91 Ross Buck, "The Gratitude of Exchange and the Gratitude of Caring."

92 Ibid., 114.

93 Mark T. Greenberg and Christa Turksma, "Understanding and Watering the Seeds of Compassion," *Research in Human Development* 12 (2015): 280-87.

94   Greenberg, "Understanding and Watering the Seeds of
     Compassion."; Laura R. Welp and Christina M. Brown, "Self-
     Compassion, Empathy, and Helping Intentions," *The Journal of
     Positive Psychology* 9, no.1 (2013): 54-65.

95   Mind and Life Education Research Network, "Contemplative
     Practices and Mental Training: Prospects for American
     Education," *Child Development Perspectives* 6 (2012): 146-53.

96   Welp, "Self-Compassion, Empathy."; Kristin D. Neff, Kristin
     L. Kirkpatrick and Stephanie S. Rude, "Self-Compassion and
     Adaptive Psychological Functioning," *Journal of Research in
     Personality* 41 (2007): 139-54.

Chapter 15

97   Wilber, *A Brief History*.

98   Matthew 6:19-21 (NIV)

99   Mufti Afzal Hoosen Elias, *Qur'aan Made Easy* (Lenasia, EDI
     Publishers, 2011).

100 Farid Mahally, "A Study of the Word 'love' in the Qur'an,"
     Answering Islam, www.answering-islam.org/Quran/Themes/love.
     htm (accessed April 2, 2016).

101 Franz Rosenzweig, *The Star of Redemption*, ed. Barbara E. Galli
     and Elliot R. Wolfson (Madison: The University of Wisconsin
     Press, 2005).

102 Ibid.

103 The Vedas are divided into four different texts that are
     considered part of the Hindu religious tradition. The texts are
     the Samhitas, Aranyakas, Brahmanas, and Upanishads. These
     are the only Indian texts that have the status of shruti meaning
     that they are perceived to be "heard" through divine revelation.
     Even so, the texts "contain new developments in theory and
     praxis over the course of almost a millennium." See: Tristan Elby,

"A Contemporary Guide to the Vedas: A Critical Survey of the Tests and Literature," *Religion Compass* 8 (2014): 128–38. The text that is primarily concerned with narratives associated with the afterlife is the Rig Veda expressed in the Upanishads, and although it is viewed as a fixed sacred text with no variations between editions, it is also considered to be deliberately ambiguous with no single interpretation. See: Gregory Shushan, "Afterlife Conceptions in the Vedas," *Religion Compass* 5 (2011): 202–13.

104 Shushan, "Afterlife Conceptions," 207.

105 1 John 4:7-8 (NIV)

106 1 John 18-19 (NIV)

107 Ephesians 1:7-8 (NIV)

108 The Trinity is not three separate gods but one God expressed by way of the unique relationship between God the Father, God the Son (Jesus), and the Holy Spirit. According to Christian theology, the Holy Spirit was sent down upon the disciples or followers of Jesus after his resurrection so that God the Father and God the Son would be present and available to all believers after the ascension of Jesus Christ into Heaven. Christians believe that the power of Christ lives on through the Holy Spirit, and that the Holy Spirit works through them to maintain a personal relationship with Jesus, to emulate the heart and mind of Christ, to demonstrate his love through works and acts of faith. Even though grace is a key element of the Christian faith and transgressions against God are forgiven, a just God still allows for consequences for those transgressions. For example, actions against the Ten Commandments, such as theft, murder, or adultery, would still require punishment here on earth even if all is forgiven by the grace of God in the spiritual realm. See: Acts 1:1–5 (NIV).

109 The Four Noble Truths are core to the teaching of Siddartha
    Gautama who is believed to be the founder of traditional
    Buddhism over 2,500 years ago. These truths point to teachings
    that suggest that 1) life is full of suffering; 2) the cause of
    suffering is our desires, longings, and attachments; 3) the
    cause of our suffering can be ended when we stop clinging to
    such desires and achieve a state of nirvana or bliss; and 4) the
    Eightfold Path which is the means by which we end suffering,
    e.g., via ethical behavior, meditation, and wisdom. See: James
    William Coleman, *The New Buddhism* (New York: Oxford
    University Press, 2001), accessed ProQuest ebrary, April 11,
    2016.

110 Ibid.

111 Gil Fronsdal, "The Buddha's Teaching on Love," Insight
    Meditation Center, http://www.insightmeditationcenter.org,
    accessed April 11, 2016.

112 Again, it is not my desire here to offer up a treatise on every
    religious perspective but to pose the deeper consideration that
    we, as a people, as indicated by these four ancient traditions, are
    innately designed to seek greater understanding of ourselves in
    relation to the world we live in, God, and ultimately love.

113 Linnell Secomb, *Philosophy and Love: From Plato to Popular
    Culture* (Edinburgh: Edinburgh University Press, 2007), 10.

114 Ibid.

115 Plato, *Symposium*, trans. Robin Waterfield, 1994:205a, in
    Philosophy and Love: From Plato to Popular Culture (Edinburgh:
    Edinburgh University Press, 2007), 12.

116 Ibid.

117 Lydia Amir, "Plato's Theory of Love: Rationality as Passion," *The
    British Journal of Philosophical Practice*, 4, no. 3 (2001), http://

www.society-for-philosophy-in-practice.org/journal/pdf/4-3%20
06%20Amir%20-%20Plato%20Love.pdf.

118   Viktor Frankl, *Man's Search for Meaning* (New York: Simon &
       Schuster, Inc., 1984).

119   Ibid., 113.

Morgan James
Speakers Group

www.TheMorganJamesSpeakersGroup.com

We connect Morgan James published authors with live and online events and audiences whom will benefit from their expertise.